I0131472

Core Teams Work
Their Principles and Practices

A Business Life Investment Model

Glen Aubrey

www.CreativeTeamPublishing.com
www.glenaubrey.com

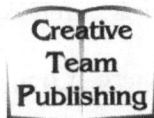

Creative
Team
Publishing

Creative Team Publishing
Ft. Worth, Texas

© 2007 by Glen Aubrey. All Rights Reserved.
Revised Edition 2019

No part of this book may be reproduced, stored in a retrieval system or transmitted in any form or by any means without the prior written permission of the publisher, except by a reviewer who may quote brief passages distributed through electronic media, or printed in a newspaper, magazine, or journal.

Disclaimers:

- Due diligence has been exercised to obtain written permission for use of references, quotes, or illustrations where required. Any additional quotes, references, or imagery may be subject to the Fair Use Doctrine. Where additional references, quotes, or imagery may require source credit, upon written certification that such a claim is accurate, credit for use will be noted on this **website: www.CreativeTeamPublishing.com.**
- The opinions and conclusions expressed are solely those of the author and/or the individuals and entities represented and are limited to the facts, experiences, and circumstances involved. No professional advice is implied, stated, or offered in any way whatsoever. You are encouraged to seek professional help, education, advice, and counsel from individuals you deem competent should you desire to learn more about how core teams work or a related topic.
- Certain names and related circumstances may have been changed to protect confidentiality. All stories where names are mentioned are used with the permission of the parties involved, if applicable. Any resemblance to past or current people, places, circumstances, or events is purely coincidental.

ISBN: 978-0-9797358-0-6
PUBLISHED BY CREATIVE TEAM PUBLISHING
www.CreativeTeamPublishing.com
Ft. Worth, Texas
Printed in the United States of America

Core Teams Work
Their Principles and Practices

A Business Life Investment Model

Glen Aubrey

*The decisions you make today
determine your audience tomorrow.*

Dedication

Core Teams Work Their Principles and Practices is dedicated to Core Teams who:

- Agree on their shared values
- Adhere to these values wholeheartedly
- Endeavor to practice their principles consistently
- Enjoy and celebrate their results

Permissions and Credits

The people who have contributed their stories and viewpoints have provided true-world examples of core team workplace challenges, opportunities, struggles, and successes. I am grateful to each one for allowing their illustration to be included in the book.

Jenafer's Introduction to Small Business used with permission of Jenafer Deyling.

Justin's First Day on the Job used with permission of Justin Aubrey.

The Story of James and Fulfilled Commitments used with permission of James Patton.

The Stovepipe used with permission of the store owners.

Working Together used with permission of Curt Marshall.

The Silo used with permission of Jim Garlow.

Word definitions taken from *The Columbia Electronic Encyclopedia* © Columbia University Press

Judy and Communication in the Media used with permission of Judy Bowen.

Growth of Your People — The Lessons of an Executive used with permission of Mary Walker.

Rob Sweet, Training Officer for Police Recruits used with permission of Rob Sweet.

The Story of Steve Annis and His Apprentice: The Investors used with permission of Steve Annis.

Table of Contents

Table of Contents

Table of Contents

Table of Contents

Getting Started —
How Much Do You Want to Grow?

The dawn rises. It's your first day on the job, and you are on time and anxious. As the new employee or employer, you've obtained this position and its accompanying title, surviving through layers of interviews, background and reference checks, intense scrutiny, and get-acquainted meetings. You'll work with some of the people you've met, others you will lead, a few will lead you, but all of them have sized you up from the moment you were introduced.

After the arduous process — sometimes exhilarating, at times exhausting — you have gained the post. So consider this: what does it mean to start well, establish strong relationships, and confront fresh but unfamiliar atmospheres, attitudes, circumstances, and controls with positive intentionality, giving your best and succeeding?

You may be new to the place but perhaps not the procedure. What should you contribute in the opening crucial moments when the honeymoon, if there is one at all, has already begun and no one has a clue how long it will last — including you?

> What does it mean to start well, establish strong relationships, and confront fresh but unfamiliar atmospheres, attitudes, circumstances, and controls with positive intentionality, giving your best and succeeding?

A fresh opportunity may pose a threat because much is unknown. In a new environment, a person searches for common threads of understanding and camaraderie or, at least, reassuring glances that indicate there are advocates, people you can trust.

On what basis will you believe someone you don't know, extend a plea for help, or request assurance during the opening hours in an unfamiliar culture? You could imagine your fate may already be determined by actions you see or by others hidden from your eyes.

Do you wonder how your performance is going to be measured or if you will be accepted? If you are the new person, regardless of position or title, how do you build a firm foundation on unproven hope, surpassing the passing whims and alleged promises, discovering your way through mazes of unknown agendas, while rising above secret alliances and the destructive person about whom you may know nothing yet?

In postmodern business climates the new guy or gal may not be taken as valuable on the basis of merit, honorable mention, pedigree, or title. In the average workplace the new person may not be granted, at least at first, open opportunity or necessary tools to succeed. The fresh face may be greeted with displays of open challenges such as, "I heard you're here because you knew the strings to pull." "Good luck... you're going to need it." Or, behind his or her back, "I wonder if he or she will make it?" "She knows the boss and made promises no one could keep." "That position should have been mine." "Let's wait and see what he is made of." Or, "I will not allow that person to succeed." In a desert scorched by relational dryness and invaded by hostile life forms, the cooling refreshment of encouragement may have long vanished with the winds of strife, skepticism, sarcastic innuendo, and barbed-wire commentary.

Even where a welcome is extended with a smile, a few well-chosen words, and the expected handshake, can you, as the new arrival, know you will experience something more than covert and consigned negatives from the ne'er-do-wells of the workplace? Is there a way to promote and dwell in a place of building up and not tearing down? If you are the one most recently arrived, is it possible to possess solid assurances that the team on which you are to serve is there to serve you, see you win, and help you succeed? How confident could you be that you will receive correct and timely information, resource tools, extended confidence, and genuine displays of, "We're glad you're here!"

Jenafer's Introduction to Small Business

"The hairdressing industry is highly competitive. When I became a licensed hairdresser just out of beauty school, I was anxious and excited. I wondered if I would be good enough to build my clientele and if I was going to be successful.

"Outward appearance is 'it' in the beauty industry. There is constant pressure to look and perform your best. My training had been extensive and I had the knowledge to become all that I wanted to be. The expectations, though high, were motivating.

"The salon I first entered provided a medium-paced place to begin my career. The biggest challenge, however, was in owning and operating my own business from the outset. I was my own promotions director, customer service provider, and administrator. From day one it was hard to figure out whom to trust and where to turn for advice.

"I obtained a mentor in the business and learned all that I could from her. I kept an open mind and retained a learning attitude. I can never think in business that I know it all. I have to constantly develop my skill and clientele to keep my business growing."

Justin's First Day on the Job

"Walking into my first day on the new job was definitely an adventure. Multiple emotions cycled their ways through me. Among them were anxiousness, nervousness, and eagerness, to name a few. I didn't know what to expect about the work or the people I'd be working with. Sure, I knew what kind of job I had applied for, but I didn't really know the full extent of what it would require of me.

"On my first day I met with one of my bosses who taught me the day-to-day procedures, explaining in greater detail what I was going to be doing. Soon after, I was handed off to one of the other workers who showed me around the place and labored alongside, explaining everything in detail.

"I was fortunate. Upon starting the work and meeting my co-workers all the 'fears' dissolved because this was an excellent group of people and they worked as a team. They drew me in as a part of them."

This is how it should work. Whether self-employed or joining the work force of an existing organization (regardless of size), experiencing a positive work environment may seem too good to be true in the opening moments of the endeavor. But it is possible. A great team is good because it is true — to its principles, and the decisions of the people on the team that promote best practices.

This is the way a core team works. Like finely meshing gears, the principles and practices of this team interlock to produce solid deliverables. Positive contributions emerge from engaged people of integrity who are part of a core team that is built on foundations of mutual support, encouragement, truthful conversations, and other values-driven behaviors.

Involvement on a core team that fits the description of health is not automatic nor should it ever be assumed. Most often a team that has achieved fitness and presents a truly welcoming environment has matured through numerous prior tests and has consistently desired something better as it has striven to reach worthwhile and desired goals — growing its members through the process.

The team that has survived and thrived has earned respect because its members have learned what to expect from the good and the bad, their successes and failures. Their actions are proof points of agreement and adherence to the **"Code of Achievement" (from *Leadership Is — How to Build Your Legacy*, (please see the website, www.CreativeTeamPublishing.com)** where their strong commitments uphold:

1. Values (the principles upon which all members agree and to which they adhere unreservedly)
2. Vision (the reasons for the team's existence)
3. Mission (the tasks the group undertakes and completes with excellence, above and beyond expectations)
4. Message (the central lessons they learn and teach to those they impact)

The core team that works well handles incidents and issues with confidence. It learns and grows through circumstances while it focuses on long term prospects because this team knows that their existence and contributions depend upon willful and values-based agreement on core principles.

Members of a great team pursue discovery of their answers to the **"Four Questions,"** from *Leadership Is —*, that **align with the "Code of Achievement"**:

1. Who are you at your core? (Values)
2. What are you called to accomplish? (Vision)
3. What do you want? (Mission)
4. Whom will you impact? (Message)

Teams in this model think and act from a solution mindset, choosing winning over whining. They engage in forming and implementing strong solutions that endure when they commit to the **"Four Decisions," as shown in** *Industrial Strength Solutions*:

1. Turn habits of complaining into habitats of construction.
2. Replace negative attitudes with positive solution-focused outlooks.
3. Redirect an ego-centered focus to concentrating on benefiting others.
4. Confront problems with positive planning and action steps.

They actively employ the **"Four Standards," from** *Industrial Strength Solutions*, **of Integrity, Decision-making, Commitment, and Faithfulness to Duty** while upholding one another in day-to-day engagements. They count character, reward competence, and celebrate good choices. Solution provision is seen in attitudes, actions, and great results.

A vitalized core team agrees with, and seeks to uphold, this first and most important truth: People are more important than what they do and relationships (decisions about another's success) come before and give rise to functions (the tasks that prove the reliability of the decisions).

A core team of people committed to exercising controlled strength is one that proves it will not be moved in its character by negative circumstances nor become subservient to compromise when confronting the challenges that come their way. Its strength originates from shared principles and sound practices. It withstands because its people have withstood while they have understood that their contributions exceed the needful functions for which their team was formed.

A team that contributes well gets jobs done from positions of internal strength, maturing while they work. Endurance permeates attitudes and activities. These people are dedicated unreservedly to trust, honoring who they are. They uphold high and verifiable accountability and employ methods that showcase consistency, obedience to values, right relationships, and examples that build legacy. These people form one great core team.

A work group embodying these positive characteristics is one with which every boss and employee looks to become engaged or associated, if — and only if — the person weighing the character of the team desires to join a group of this kind for the right reasons, wholeheartedly desiring to contribute to its success.

If you are the new person, would you like to join a team like this? If you are the recently hired boss, would you like to lead a team like this? Regardless of your current position, title, or tenure, would you like to help create and work with a team like this?

What makes a team work well—or, better put—what makes a great team far exceed mediocre expectations? In two companion volumes already referenced, *Leadership Is —* and *Industrial Strength Solutions*, leadership is described as not inherited, but chosen, and teams that make positive and long-lasting contributions are shown to accomplish their goals because what they want is based on solid beliefs in unshakeable truths. These two books explain and illustrate that simply following "easy-way" instructions and check-off lists will not necessarily produce greatness if building lasting legacies of contribution are the higher goals of interaction.

Leadership Is — How to Build Your Legacy,
Industrial Strength Solutions Build Successful Work Teams!
and *Core Teams Work Their Principles and Practices*
are books written by Glen Aubrey and published by
Creative Team Publishing.
Please visit www.CreativeTeamPublishing.com to order.

Great core teams work well because they are composed of growing people, firmly convinced that achieving leadership team creation and cooperation constitute ideals of completion that require diligence and hard work. They know that efforts to acquire what they desire are worth the expenditures they require of themselves. These teams produce better people as part of the process and don't use them up. When what they receive endures beyond the price the team paid to realize its dreams, they've won.

Gregory Edwards, the New Manager

After many years of working in his chosen profession, Greg received what he thought would be the position of his dreams, joining a dedicated staff for a respected enterprise. He was responsible to senior executive management. He worked remotely from home, his duties seemed to fit him well, and travel was minimal. Staff assigned to him consisted of administrative assistants and sub-contractors, as well as on-site managers for those times when Greg needed to be at the company's home office. Responsibilities aligned with his creative solution thinking. Challenges appeared to be manageable and he set about fulfilling his role with enthusiasm.

There was one problem, though. Russell, Greg's immediate supervisor, was hungry for power, position, and prestige. He lorded it over his staff with unmitigated fervor—especially in group meetings. While Russell talked frequently about teams and how much he valued a team approach, to Greg it became blatantly clear in short order that what Russell *did* was not in line with what he *said*.

As initial weeks dissolved into opening months, Greg realized that working for Russell was not going to work unless behaviors changed. Greg came to the conclusion that this professional relationship was anything but a team. This was a dictatorship run by an insecure leader whose chosen modes of operation consisted of intimidation, interruption, unclear communication, and subversive, behind-the-scenes maneuvering.

Interestingly, the CEO for whom Russell worked treated his executive staff the same way.

Striving from within to forge values into a working environment that clearly needed help, Greg sought to bridge communication gaps on his own team, confront problems appropriately, and stimulate staff growth and development.

Russell had a lot to deal with in Greg. Here was an employee who was clearly liked and respected because he did what he said he was going to do. His product delivery was on time and on target. He showed respect to his co-workers and endeavored to produce a team that worked well. Were Russell to have been more secure and appreciative he would have sensed, if not completely understood, that enfolding Greg instead of stifling him would have been a best choice. But Russell didn't get it. Instead of promoting creative freedom, Russell employed his tough and testy traits of put-downs, gossip, and power-center positioning. Russell feared that Greg would become the go-to guy, so he tried to reign in what he though was a threat, but he couldn't have been more incorrect in his assessment and action.

Greg could see Russell's discomfiture from nearly the first day. His efforts to bridge the gaps and cooperate with Russell were refused — not once, but repeatedly. The staff saw it and was not sure how to handle it. But executive leadership above Russell actually encouraged even more disconnect, as though distance and distrust were the characteristics to be admired and acquired. It was unbelievable.

Enough became enough after nearly a year of constant struggle and, with no end to the dilemma in sight, Greg resigned. It was a good decision and it was handled well—at least on Greg's part. While not burning bridges, Greg did venture to tell the truth within an attitude of respect to Russell and the company's leader. Communication with both of these men bore little fruit at the time but future events proved that this was a good choice. In a few months the CEO resigned in disgrace and Russell soon moved on to greater responsibilities in another company, but Russell and Greg maintained occasional friendly contact.

Ties hammered out in unfortunate circumstances still bind Russell and Greg today and may last a lifetime. Their shared relationship is mutually beneficial even though they are not engaged in the same enterprise or industry.

In tough times, when truth and principles are upheld, they can produce benefits even if won through difficulty. Relationships founded on principle endure beyond what may appear to be ineffectual results at the moment—if practiced on the basis of truth and respect, regardless.

Core Teams Work Their Principles and Practices is the third in a series of three books, presenting practical application of principles that, when exercised consistently, validate the worth of solid and true foundations and provide frameworks and proofs for repeatable operations that produce consistent quality.

All three books, ***Core Teams Work Their Principles and Practices, Industrial Strength Solutions Build Successful Work Teams!,*** and ***Leadership Is— How to Build Your Legacy,*** are business life investment models that you are invited to use in your workplace. These three books compose a coordinated study for workgroups of any size.

Great core teams work well because they are composed of growing people, firmly convinced that achieving leadership team creation and cooperation constitute ideals of completion that require diligence and hard work. They know that efforts to acquire what they desire are worth the expenditures they require of themselves. These teams produce better people as part of the process and don't use them up. When what they receive endures beyond the price the team paid to realize its dreams, they've won.

Core Teams Work Their Principles and Practices is the third in the series of three books—presenting practical applications of principles that, when exercised consistently, validate the worth of solid and true foundations and provide frameworks and proofs for repeatable operations that produce quality consistently. All three books, ***Core Teams Work Their Principles and Practices, Industrial Strength Solutions Build Successful Work Teams!,*** and ***Leadership Is— How to Build Your Legacy,*** are business life investment models that you are invited to use in your life and workplace.

This book explores the principles and practices of a Core Team, illustrating how values, when applied to the working environment, change it for the better.

- The opening you are reading now, **Getting Started — How Much Do You Want to Grow?** is preceded by the pages on which the **Dedication**, **Permissions and Credits**, and **Table of Contents** appear.

- **Chapter 1: On Time, on Target, on Treasure** examines these elements of success.

- **Chapter 2: Maui's Haleakala — A Study on Perspective** comprises a study on viewpoints. Healthy teams possess many perspectives and learn how to use them wisely.

- **Chapter 3: A Clean Atmosphere Is Made of Fresh Air** confronts the characteristics of the micromanager, the intimidator, and the attention-grabber, and explains how to handle stress.

- **Chapter 4: Truth and Tenacity** describes these important healthy team characteristics. A wise team embraces both.

- **Chapter 5: Stovepipes, Silos, and the Circle of Rights** views two challenging workplace phenomena, showing that isolationism and working together are opposed. When you are the right person in the right place you know that you fit with the others on your team on the basis of shared and agreed values. Diversity is welcomed and contributes to strength when the mixes of people, ideas, and production are supportive.

- In **Chapter 6: Team Communication — Examples that Endure** the all-important topic of communication takes center stage. In this "how to do it better" chapter you will read methods of conducting profitable conversations and productivity meetings, the value of communication loop closure, the importance of confidentiality and obtaining permission, and the expectations from growing your people.

- **Chapter 7: Rehearsal and Performance — A Customer Service Model** describes core team customer service initiatives based on enduring principles.

- **Chapter 8: Reserves, Not Reservations** identifies and addresses the reservoirs of values that healthy core teams possess and shows how they may be used.

- In **Chapter 9: You Can Bank on It** the benefits of investing in the people of the core team are examined and illustrated, as well as the returns on their investments.

- In **Chapter 10: Core Issues for Core Teams** the 21 most common issues, challenge points, and related solutions of a core team are tallied, explained, and cross-referenced.

- CTRG's **Relationship, Operational Structure Analysis (ROSA)** is presented and explained.

- The final section, **Concluding: The "Secrets" of Success Are Calls to Action** shows that many so-called concealed success principles are no longer hidden to a team that truly wants to operate within the benefits of *Core Teams Work Their Principles and Practices.* Three hundred twenty-one principles and practices are listed. It is up to you and me to turn these ideals into ideas and action steps.

- **Acknowledgements** are located just before the CTRG information page and are expressed from a heart of thanks.
- **A description of Creative Team Resources Group, Inc. (CTRG)** wraps up the book. You are invited to contact our organization for speaking engagements, consultation services, and related tools to help you and your teams succeed.

Strong bridges are constructed between a value and its corresponding validating actions when principles are intentionally learned and earnestly lived. Because learning becomes living only when behaviors change, each section of the book is crafted to teach and then reach beyond instruction into real-life environments of the workplace, the testing and proving grounds of principles in practice. It is "on the job" that truth presented is truth perceived and applied where it really counts.

Most people enjoy a story that proves a point. Interspersed throughout the book are true accounts that show evidence of principled activities or the lack of them. These stories come from people in multiple sectors of society and work experiences. The fields represented are listed below in alphabetical order:

- Arts
- Camping
- City Government
- Construction
- Cosmetology
- County Government
- Entrepreneurial enterprises
- Farming
- Financial services
- Investments
- Household products and cleaning services
- Law enforcement
- Manufacturing
- Marketing
- Media communications
- Military
- Music production
- Non-profit organizations
- Parks and recreation
- Property management
- Real estate
- Religion
- Retail and wholesale sales and customer services
- Small business
- State Government
- Theater
- United States Federal Government
- Warehousing
- Wholesale distribution

True stories from identifiable sources have been included with the explicit permissions of the parties involved. Other true stories for which permission was not obtained are included because they proved the point so well. For these illustrations, the names and incidents have been changed. Any resemblance within them to any known entity, company, person, incident or issue, is purely coincidental.

At points within the book a text box is placed containing questions for your team. These insertions are designed to serve as discussion points for your group, to encourage application of principles you have just read.

If you were recently the new person on the new job, or one who welcomed a previously unknown individual, consider this as you begin: What principles and practices would you like your core team to demonstrate so that your team's work culture is altered for the better? Further, what part would *you* like to play to achieve the worthwhile goals of building greater people, superior contribution, positive results, and living legacy — at the same time?

The answers to these questions are vital. You are invited to allow the principles and practices to reveal your responsibilities and position you to become the learner or the leader, but above all, the living example of one who decides and acts.

Enjoy the journey. Let's get started.

What principles and practices would you like your core team to demonstrate so that your team's work culture is altered for the better? Further, what part would you like to play to achieve the worthwhile goals of building greater people, superior contributions, positive results, and living legacies — all at the same time?

Chapter 1:
On Time, on Target, on Treasure

Time, target, and treasure — these are three necessities for success. Combined, they provide incentive, encourage action, and supply relational and functional measurements. They are powerful, life-sustaining endowments when exercised well or incredibly destructive enemies of a team's success when utilized poorly.

Time, target, and treasure cooperate to produce solid results when they are diligently employed from the right motives. They are strong as individual contributors but mighty when engaged together. Used wisely, time, target, and treasure position right people for the right reasons and yield exceptional reward.

A core team looks for opportunities to use well the one-chance only resource of time. When time is used to focus on the right target, the team produces value-added treasure in its process of engagement and crafts opportunities for earned celebrations when the job is over. The core team that works together well makes effective use of these success points because the team is attuned to their roots and causes, their values, vision, mission, and message. These elements bind them toward building themselves and their production. The team who understands the right use of time, target, and treasure produces more than what may be expected for less than it costs to engage them.

A group of individuals who may work together but are not yet a core team may function because they have to, drawn into required tasks apart from an understanding and application of higher motives. These persons may not yet realize how crucial time utilization is, or how life-sustaining knowing and reaching their targets will be. They may not yet have the appreciation that tangible rewards — treasures — will surely follow their efforts, regardless of size. Perhaps they'll learn that underutilized people can become far greater resources to a business when the leaders invest in them and encourage their growth.

What kind of a team would you prefer to serve on or lead? A team that demonstrates disciplines in best-uses of time, identifies and stays focused on agreed targets, and sees treasures revealed in the processes and product? Or one that merely copes and hopes, and barely succeeds, if at all, disconnected from resourcefully engaging time, target, and treasure? Clearly, if you are a person who wants to be part of, or lead a working and productive core team, you would choose the former.

Target

The Core Team's
Resources:
The Elements of
Success

Time   **Treasure**

Evaluate the team on which you serve. In consideration of the most effective utilization of these three elements of success, how does it measure up? What action steps would you compose or propose that would contribute to making your team better in people and production, if it could be shown that better time management, target focusing, and treasure stewardship could be employed?

Underutilized people can become far greater resources to a business when the leaders invest in them and encourage their growth.

Time

Think about time, and you quickly realize it's made up of far more than a memory of how you've spent it. Time, once used, is gone—what remains are the results of your choices. What you really have to consider is what you want to make of the time you have left.

Some people think that the older a person becomes the quicker time flies, and its progression accelerates when you are having fun. Time, while not a variable, is treated in varying ways, some to profit and others to loss. The time spender makes the decision of how to use it.

The user is wholly in charge of time's profit potential, whether invested or squandered. The seeds of decisions, whether energies consume or magnify what they reach and seize, reside within a person's judgments. Circumstances are not sole determining factors of success or failure. The use of time, seen in profitable or detrimental rewards, is determined by choice. Choices produce fate and, ultimately, destiny.

Embracing the responsibility of spending quality time in productive ways causes the bearer to ask certain revealing questions about the activities that consume your time:

1. Is time consideration important to you and if not, why?
2. How do you prioritize your time for learning and output?
3. How balanced is your time relative to family, work, and relaxation?

4. Are you on time?
5. If you are not on time, how many other people's time assets are you wasting?
6. In how many ways might your work activities not honor another core team member's time?
7. Is time a burden or a benefit?
8. How much of your time management failure is someone else's fault, according to you?
9. If you consider that you use time well, what do you show for its use that lasts beyond it?
10. Does your time utilization build up those around you, and how do they know?
11. If you were to define "wasted time," what would your definition be?
12. How dedicated are you to spending quality time on any engagement so you know you are best prepared to deliver well?

Unique opportunities to engage and invest come daily. Once consumed, the time it takes to recognize, evaluate, decide, and act upon these opportunities — as well as the time to enjoy their results — is history forever.

Once you reach beyond now, that portion of your story is written. This realization should cause you, if you are serious about turning resources into results, to become more conscientious about method as well as motive.

So many people waste resources without considering consequences. Whether seen or not seen, resources — time included — are too often simply cast away on the winds of "I don't care." Born of a profound lack of responsibility, folks in this mindset decide to not treat resources as precious, no matter what they are: wildlife, money, forests, mountains, rivers, wetlands, beaches, family, friends, quiet moments, learning opportunities, fun, finances, or time. In other words, time-wasting is not an isolated characteristic; it is part of a struggling character.

What is time worth and how is it evaluated? Many professionals put a price on their time, and they should. The more expensive the invoice, the more value the service provider attaches to the use of this resource. No problem with that theory. But what about the people on a team who waste time and, in the process, cause other people to throw away theirs as a consequence? Who accounts for this toss and who should be responsible for its loss?

There are many ways of judging levels of dedication regarding the use and usefulness of time. Treating time as a precious commodity, core team members use markers as verifications of faithfulness. The core team member who wants to use time well will:

1. Show up early to a job and when the official clock starts won't still be getting settled.

2. Not begin to pack up and prepare to leave before fulfilling a day's obligations, demonstrating he or she is less concerned about the moment of departure and more committed to faithful completion of responsibility.

3. Not be so dedicated to keeping minutia-track of the minute-to-minute, that what is received by the

employer merely equates to a bare minimum of what is expected.

4. Go beyond what is required to what is inspired in fulfillment of duty, showing that time well spent produces positive and lasting effects.

5. Make sure that compensated time represents faithfully completed tasks.

6. Produce results that build toward future growth because current tasks have been fulfilled with excellence.

7. Not evaluate success or failure, worth or wealth, on the basis of time's expenditure alone; rather, on the collective fruits of what has been produced that will endure beyond its expenditure.

Time is an ally to those who use it with an attitude of allegiance to solid core values and the growth of the core team. Time well spent builds a framework of engagement and is never used as an excuse for abandonment of responsible action. To those who may say, "I really need to..." but don't act upon the need or don't put a required duty on a calendar for accomplishment, time use is evaluated more in terms of convenience and comfort instead of providing focused motivation toward fulfillment.

A core team participant who uses time faithfully will take initiative to publish a calendar to other core team members of how his or her time will be spent so that faithful demonstration to duty and completion of obligation is not hidden, supposed, or assumed; rather, it is declared and accountably upheld. If time utilization is important, then the right people should know the facts and factors of business-related time use. Appropriate non-confidential accessibility should be granted to those who need to know, as opposed to being hidden so that others have to chase it down.

Bottom line: If a core team leader, department manager, project administrator, or other rightfully interested person feels the obligation to manage another's time because that person can't or won't manage his or her own time faithfully, then that collection of proofs must be handled in a way composed of one or more of these actions:

1. Teach appropriate time management.
2. Model effective time use.
3. Calendar appropriately.
4. Publish a calendar to those who need to see it.
5. Instruct the worker how to take initiative in reporting time utilization.
6. Correct time mismanagement in obedience to a prescribed and mutually agreed method.
7. Impose time restrictions if a team member proves unfaithful in his or her use of time.
8. Celebrate positive behavioral changes when time utilization and project fulfillment successes are evidenced.

Creating workplace atmospheres of healthy time application does not constrict innovation, nor does it conflict with trust paradigms around which great core teams build and function. In fact, on healthy teams the need for effective time management will be a welcomed opportunity to prove agreement to core team ideals. Solid teams not only don't shy away from time reporting — they welcome it.

This truth says a lot about those who don't want to reveal their time utilization or calendar, who resist faithful reporting, who are reticent or refuse to showcase how they spend their energies. Faithful accountability does not avoid truth-telling — it initiates it.

Proper time utilization is a fact to be known and shown. The person dedicated to faithful accountability demonstrates a proactive stance to use well that which is consumed only once. This person generates more for time's expenditure and creates a model of engagement that other team members, if they desire greatness, want to exemplify. Everyone on a team wins more when time is engaged well.

Target

My son, Justin, and I participate in target shooting on occasion. It's an activity we thoroughly enjoy, and we employ various types of guns when we go. I am amazed at his accuracy with the 12-gauge shotgun as well as an assorted array of pistols and rifles — the latter especially with scopes. We value the experience for more than just the fun it includes when the targets are hit squarely, not just grazed slightly or missed. Hitting the object at its dead-center point is quite exciting.

Targets are identifying marks of evaluation. They provide focus points of action and undeniable evaluations of success or failure once an action is completed.

In business cultures where demands for output are constant, targets must be identified and kept at the forefront of concentration—both in understanding and undertaking. Ask yourself and your core team what your targets are and how you will reach them. How does your team know they have accomplished the goals which the targets represent?

Many years ago Justin and I went fishing at a local mountain lake, part of which was being drained at the time. We asked the forest ranger where the best fishing was for a couple of novices, and the gentleman replied that the prime spot was near a small dam where the drainage point was located. This was a place where, according to him, the lake trout weighing about 2.5 to 3 pounds would fight like 5-pounders, and he virtually promised we would catch something if we were lucky. I guess that's always the case!

Reaching the appointed place we did what any fisherman would do: baited the hook with a worm, cast the line, and waited. And we didn't have to wait long. In fact, the pace of success was unnerving as well as exciting, almost beyond belief. We caught so many fish so quickly it was almost embarrassing—not to us, but to the well-seasoned fishing sportsmen positioned within yards of us, who were engaged in the same activity but not enjoying our results. Our success was so prompt and plentiful that soon some of these avid fishermen approached us, asking with smiles, but really-wanting-to-know attitudes, "What is your secret?" This was just too good of a moment to let pass without having some fun, so we milked it for all it was worth.

"Well," I said furtively, glancing around to make sure no one else would hear, "you take a worm, like this ... and put it on a hook, like this ... cast the line out, like this ...." It was an obvious lesson from a rookie that to the weather-beaten and experience-laden fishing aficionados was "old hat," of course. I knew the game was up when one of the men asked, "What are you fishing for?" and I replied, "Anything we catch." Smiles were exchanged, but it remained true we had caught the most fish that day in certainly the least amount of time—in fact more than we could eat while still under the limit. It was a great and pleasurable moment for dad and son, a good ending to a fish story where none of them got away. But this story is not only about fishing.

In competitive market-placed business environments, rarely, if at all, does the luck of the hook, worm, line, and cast result in something more than wasted effort and worthless consequence when effort that appears to be right is expended without a target present. Luck, if it exists, may depend more on right placement of efforts seen in due diligence, consisting of study and preparation, than simply mere chance. Blessing may fall into somewhat the same category.

Have you heard the story of the farmer and the country church preacher? It was a Friday after a busy week of crop cultivation, and the preacher came to call. The farmer, wiping his brow, and grateful that the work day was finished, leaned on a fence rail and chewed on a piece of flax. When the preacher approached, both gazed upon the farmer's well-groomed fields where a bountiful harvest was ready for reaping, rows upon rows of rich earth and luscious crops. In a moment of heartfelt gratitude for the plenteous produce, the preacher proclaimed, "Look at what God has given you!" The farmer, nodding, paused a second and thoughtfully replied, "You should have seen these fields when they were just God's."

Nothing in that story denies that blessings come. You have not lived very long if you have not seen blessings that may appear without apparent cause. What the story says, however, is this: Desired results originate not only from possessing opportunity, but also from downright hard work to make the opportunity become reality. Dedicated labor is necessary, not just for raising crops but for realizing any success. Hard work applied to a primary target is surer to succeed than hard work applied to no target at all.

It therefore comes as no unique revelation that possessing a target and utilizing hard work to achieve its goals are part of the same needful slate of action steps. One may exist without the other, but, in combination, positive results and commensurate rewards are realized.

Count your blessings. Be grateful. Also be diligent, understanding that what you reap is likely a direct result of what you've sown. Targets are vital to the realization of success. Combined with time, they become vital measurements of profitable ends. Often these results are described as treasures — but treasure, while it includes profit, is much more than what you may wind up taking to the bank.

Treasure

In these two books, *Leadership Is—* and *Industrial Strength Solutions,* an end-product's viable worth is seen in helping grow better people and the solutions they provide. When great people are provisioned through strong relationships and superior functions they should achieve monetary and other measurable gains as well as increased maturity.

Treasure is not hidden when it is a motivator. Indeed, it is fully disclosed and projected. It is part of preparation and the product of due diligence. It's the result of successful efforts born and nourished from agreed values and commensurate activity. A team without a treasure in view is a team that may work but see no reason for their labor apart from a paycheck. But there is more.

Treasure is uniquely tied to values (the principles upon which collective agreement exists), vision (the reasons why an organization is formed and functions), mission (the activities of the group and their measurements), and message (the life-lessons learned and taught). Treasure is evidenced as both an intangible and tangible asset.

Treasure is intangible when it refers to people's value because of who they are—not just what they produce. This treasure is all about internal worth that, when positioned correctly and encouraged consistently, produces long-lasting returns. Treasuring people is integral to active and positive relationships. It is shown in how people are treated where desires to promote holistic development contribute to great decisions about another person's success. Within this definition people are honored, dignity is upheld, respect is a living characteristic of interaction, and trust and integrity are integrated fully into daily activity.

Treasure is tangible where it is manifested in concrete rewards for efforts expended. Money, profit, items, goods, and services are examples. These treasures are the touchable assets that proper functioning provides. They are essential to a thriving commerce and provide benefits for the people who engage in productive work.

What is needed is balance between the character of the intangible treasure and the compensation of the tangible one. One may exist without the other but, like hard work and targets, they are better when they cooperate. Treasures that are only intangible may produce good feelings but insufficient or inconclusive action; treasures that are exclusively tangible may produce money and means while inappropriately consuming the people who do the production, much like killing the goose that lays the golden egg.

Treasure, to be balanced and complete, considers and includes the people and their products. Not hidden, but known and acquired, balanced treasure is both unseen and seen.

Treasure that can't be handled or touched by one of the five senses is hard to quantify, but all participants on a core team know when the intangible assets of trust, assurance, confidence, integrity, honor, faithfulness, and commitment are absent or have never been part of the DNA of a group.

Conversely, a team knows when these intangibles are present in workable and productive motives and methods, exemplified by a group that possesses and utilizes their strengths.

Tangible treasure comes from best decisions to incorporate best actions on the basis of best motives, to build people and production, in that order. This process is more honored, valued, and highly prized than one that rests on luck, inappropriate treatment of personnel, inconsiderate or manipulative tactics, or worse.

Treasure that is part of a holistic understanding of people and provision is truly esteemed and earned. It promotes balance in its people and what they produce. "On Treasure" is both a dedication to measured and meaningful growth and the result of a process of achievement. It is good for one who wants treasure to be the hallmark of effective effort, to see evidences of its existence — intangibly and tangibly. Consider these noticeable measures of its presence:

1. People are treated as valuable consistently, from the start of a project, during phases of implementation and achievement, all the way through to its conclusion.

2. Intangible assets, known as values (principles), represent recurring ideas in discussions, evaluations, corrections, and celebrations.

3. Treasures are fully disclosed; there are no hidden agendas. This disclosure is part of advance planning, sharing ideas, action proposals, the actions themselves, and the commensurate reward systems.

4. Intangible and tangible treasures are not used manipulatively for gain at the expense of any team member.

5. Treasures, both unseen and seen, are used to position people for success, not demean or sacrifice them on altars of selfishness. They are certainly not employed to intimidate the very people who help tangible assets come into being.

6. Tangible treasures are amassed. Utilization of their accumulation may include investing or giving them away in appropriate times and settings where benefits outweigh and outlast the value of the treasures themselves.

7. Tangible treasures and the valued people who produce them enhance their collective worth. Together, they contribute to more than pecuniary profit when they encourage growing people and production simultaneously.

A core team that is on time, on target, and on treasure is one that performs well because it is well-formed. Solid formation provides lasting foundations for a team's contributions that thrive on merits unseen and seen — appropriately apportioning resources and matching efforts with known end-deliverables in sight, while building the people, enjoying the processes, and benefiting from the profits their contributions produce.

William and the Vacuum of Dependability

It was long past the regular hour of departure and way beyond a normal level of expectation when the entire team, except William, decided to finish no matter what. Several weeks prior, they had committed themselves to completing a job they had known would be time-consuming and energy-draining. Even before the project was initiated they had figured that finishing well would take mountains of extra effort — they just hadn't known to what degree, but they had all agreed to see it through with excellence.

Now, in the final moments of completion, time and significant money were in play. Requirements warred against tired but determined spirits. These individuals had declared themselves committed to this cause; indeed, the members believed this dedication was shared by the whole team because all had stated they were in it to the end.

But William proved them wrong. Unbelievably, at the last hour, he decided to leave the inter-related job actions, fully realizing that much — if not total — success for a completed project depended on his contributions. When he announced his departure his team leader was profoundly surprised.

Asking William to reiterate his departure declaration to be sure he fully understood, the core team leader even took the opportunity in front of the members to restate it back to William, to assure total group comprehension of what was about to occur. William had decided that he was going home because he had an early morning engagement unrelated to this project. His priorities conflicted with those of the group, unknown to any before this moment. Leaving everyone up in the air in what already was a late night endeavor when they were so close to completion shocked and upset the rest of his team.

After William unceremoniously departed, duty assignments were shifted, roles redefined and responsibilities in new formats engaged. The group rallied. Their energies became even more focused. They worked harder, and a little longer. They would not give up.

The project was completed that night — on time, ahead of budget, and with excellence, in spite of William's exit. Further, as future events would show, it would bring expansive rewards, building confidence and profitable compensation to the core team who produced it.

When William showed up for work at the next regularly scheduled core team operation, two days after his unwarranted and untimely departure, he was terminated. His feigned surprise at this dismissal was another demonstration of just how disconnected he had become. While job abandonment constituted cause enough for his firing, his supposed failure to understand the hardship into which he had plunged his whole team by his lack of dependability was tantamount to incredulous.

William did not value the time commitments of the other team members, he clearly was not on target with job completion responsibility, and he showcased a devastating devaluing of treasure — in the people of his team and the product they had agreed to produce. Great core teams recognize that elements of time, target, and treasure are necessities of success, that the departure of any countermands the success of the others.

Great teams assure that three factors of achievement — better people, greater products, and increased profit — are present, realized for their worth, appropriately engaged, and evaluated consistently for what they should produce. Without time, target, and treasure in play, the goal of completion with excellence is harder to achieve, especially when a hardened heart reveals inadequate and compromising character.

Chapter 2:
Maui's Haleakala —
A Study on Perspective

The road to Hana from Kaanapali, on the island of Maui, Hawaii, is hair-pin winding, composed of what seems to be an unending array of twists and turns. Driving them consumes three to four hours, depending on how often you stop to enjoy the truly beautiful waterfalls, beaches, fruit stands, and invigorating scenery. Upon arrival at your destination you tend to forget about the drive — almost. You certainly become fascinated with the town of Hana, and ten miles farther down the road you may quench your quest for adventure with a hike to the Seven Pools. This trip is worth it and, as many will tell you, so is the swim in the pools.

But about half way through approximately 500 sharp curves, it might have dawned on you, if you are the driver or a passenger who is susceptible to motion sickness, that at some point you have to return the way you came. Taking a full day of behind-the-wheel concentration to get there and back may be daunting for even the most experienced and dedicated type-A motivated "we *will* see all of this" tourist. However, most who have taken the trip (and I would be one of these) will tell you that it's good — in spite of the duration, the drive, and the distance. This journey holds vast storehouses of creative camera shots and treasured memories that validate your experience.

Rarely, however, do people take the opportunity to return on a forbidden and more difficult road, by going around the other side of the island. This roadway is declared "off limits" to regular vehicles, especially rented ones. I have taken the trip once on this risky pathway, encompassing the whole of Maui. Not only did the difficult drive become an added venture, the trip, with its new (to my eyes) vistas and unpopulated landscapes, was nothing short of breathtaking—and a little scary, too. During the moments when our group traversed roadways where sections were clearly not friendly or completely safe for traffic, I wondered if we had made a good choice to negotiate this return. This heightened danger is one reason why extreme caution and obedience to conditions, along with securing necessary permissions and appropriate vehicles, is essential if one wants to travel the east side road. Driver, be wary. This trip will be completed at your own risk.

Should you experience the around-the-island journey, you will notice the differences in the landscapes from the road from Kaanapali to Hana, and the road far less traveled for coming back. On this new venture you are fully circling Haleakala, an extinct volcanic mountain. While the road to Hana from Kaanapali washes your eyes with lush and overwhelming vistas of green, crystal waterfalls with surging streams and ponds, and a bountiful abundance of tropical life, on the other side of the island your senses are greeted with far different revelations. Framed by the ocean on your left, in places the backside of the mountain appears utterly devoid of life. Punctuated with cracked folds of earth in silent historic rocky cascades, you can only imagine the mighty forces of eruption that sent molten material plunging down the mountain and into the sea, crossing the very path you have chosen to take. This volcano's fury had forged its own underground shafts, released its destruction skyward, and then rolled like an atomic blast as it reached toward watery graves, clutching and discarding all that had dared to stand in its way.

Dwell on this enough and an enlivening sense of reality as to perspective may cross your mind—it's the same mountain but a wholly different view. It's the same volcano but a brand new truth. The mountain hasn't changed but your outlook has.

Perspective changes the way an object is seen but doesn't alter it. Reaction to perspective is that state where decisions are made, coming from an intake of facts and feelings, investigating and then combining them to create a grid of evaluation where choices are framed. It is in this sifting and decision-making process that true character is revealed, values are known and weighed, and actions originate.

Core teams value differences in perspective when considering best action courses for fulfillment of necessary tasks. Variety is vitality when it motivates due diligence. A great core team realizes that apart from thorough deliberation, a less than desirable choice may be made.

Opportunities become viable options when varied perspectives are weighed as part of the process of decision making. Strength is a by-product of thoughtful and respectful deliberation where people's views are ascertained, explained, and evaluated in atmospheres of trust, loyalty, truth-telling and responsible ownership.

Consider these questions:

1. What are your team's perspectives and how does the group sift and scrutinize them?
2. If you are the engaged and motivating leader, or an active member who is interested in your people and their processes, what is your responsibility in processes of discovery?
3. What are the lines of demarcation that you use to view varying perspectives to gain best ideas that, when activated, result in preferred deliverables?
4. How open are you and your team to set aside necessary time and collective resources to participate in group gatherings and discussions where differing outlooks are presented with openness, encouragement, non-judgmental attitudes, and mutual respect?

There are inhibitors to open expressions of perspective, of course. Some come from circumstances, but most often they arise from less-than-convinced people, who usually are themselves less than convincing. These are the folks who impede innovation. Hiding like cockroaches until the light of a new idea reveals them, they hurry to scuttle change, creep up to scare innovation, bother the committed, and shy away from creativity. Thankfully, it doesn't take too long to discover them and a great core team won't tolerate their negativity for too long.

People who are threatened by other core team member's perspectives possess unique characteristics. When rays of open and forthright discussion shine on them, they are tough to motivate and slow to consider opinions if different from their own. They express concerns couched in what appear on the surface to be well-meaning expressions, but engaged discussion may reveal more true intentions.

Resistance to consideration of other's ideas can be either covert or overt. When covert, the adverse individual usually makes his or her process of prevention known in defensive body language, negative attitudes, or biting innuendo. It's a kind of negativity that becomes insidious when it is falsely masked in worry about the "direction the team is taking" or other insincere phrases.

In overt demonstrations, tell-tale words and disengaging signs are offered by people who are reticent or remote, who refuse both openly and behind the scenes to engage in open dialogue and discovery-related sharing of perspectives.

Words and phrases:

1. "We have always done it the other way."
2. "Another new idea that will fail — like all the others."
3. "This is my responsibility, my turf. No need to change anything."
4. "I am not comfortable with looking at alternatives."
5. "No."
6. "If it ain't broke, don't fix it."

7. "There is no reason to go through yet another discovery stage — what we're doing is okay for what is required."

8. "I am not interested in leading any new team or project."

9. "Sure, whatever you say — but let me tell you I will not be part of anything that looks like it's failing."

10. "Stay under the radar. No one will notice."

11. "Do whatever it takes to not make waves."

12. "I don't care."

13. "This exercise is a waste of time."

14. "I'm not interested. Good luck in finding someone who is."

15. "It won't work."

Signs and signals:

1. The non-engaged person is late to meetings where open discovery conversations are to take place, or misses group gatherings entirely, offering poor excuses.

2. Smug attitudes substitute for sincere attention.

3. History proves that words and actions are not followed through.

4. Communication loops are not closed.

5. Assigned tasks are ignored, slow to be accomplished, or discussed with less than enthusiastic input, yielding commensurate inept output.

6. After given specific tasks, the negligent person has to be chased down to see what — if anything — is

happening toward the conclusion of an established goal.

7. Mediocrity is a norm.
8. Confrontation replaces cooperation.
9. Evaluations are strained in processes and conclusions.
10. The negative person shows divided or diminishing loyalty.
11. New ideas are greeted with questioning glances, discouraging frowns, outward intimidation, rolling eyes, or behind-the-back disagreement or disruption.
12. The disparaging party thwarts progress if the new and agreed idea was not his or her concept to begin with. This disgruntled and disengaged person displays desires to impede accelerated momentum.
13. Whining replaces a willingness to try because a fear of failure rules.
14. When considering fresh thoughts and new plans, risk-avoidance takes the place of desire.
15. Misery seeks its own company and fosters disunity from its associations.

In contrast, open participation in expressing perspectives is one of the viable and vital signs of communicative life and group health. In this state, fresh and engaging ideas are purposefully presented, collected, and evaluated and eventually contribute to decisive action steps.

How does your core team handle discovery? Where true longing exists to appropriately consider other member's views, positive traits will characterize your team's perspective discussions.

If your group's values include people's growth, stimulated creativity, sincere motivation, and upward movement toward fulfilling its goals with excellence, then you should witness and participate in some of these demonstrations in conversation:

1. "What a great idea!" (This exclamation is expressed with sincerity and the history of engagement to prove it.)
2. "If we consider this course, then Teams A and B will collaborate — they can share their strengths and allocate responsibilities to accomplish the goal."
3. "This course of action will stretch us. Let's consider it."
4. "I'll own it."
5. "Just because our old system has worked doesn't mean we should not consider change in light of this new opportunity."
6. "If new methods demonstrate they could work, then we will overcome the challenges they might include."
7. "What is needed here may not be solved by the traditional methods. Let's look at fresh ones."
8. "Let's try it."
9. "We can do this. We should do this. We will do this."
10. "Let me outline the plan and submit it for your review."
11. "I'll help."
12. "Consider it done."
13. "I would like to be part of this new venture."

14. "This will work!"
15. "Well done!"

You might also witness or help to initiate these actions:

1. Core team members request, receive, or design and distribute agendas in advance of a perspective discovery meeting, are on time or early to its appointed place, and are already interacting when the meeting is called to order. Anticipation in the room is high and contagious.

2. Interest is overt and breeds additional innovation as discussion proceeds. Initial criticisms are few.

3. Affirmation and appreciation are openly given and gratefully received.

4. Openness and encouragement are trademarks of engagement. There is no intimidation in these exchanges.

5. Assignments are welcomed, if not requested.

6. Tasks are performed well, ahead of timeline requirements, and communicated as to process and fulfillment to the people who need to know.

7. Excellence is the standard the team employs. Its products are not only noteworthy, they are noticed and celebrated.

8. Evaluations are seen as welcomed opportunities to continue down paths of heightened provision.

9. Correction, when needed, is done objectively, separating the person from the function.

10. Cooperation in charting next-phases of enhanced and enduring productivity is clearly evidenced.

11. Attuned people show they are interested through asking timely questions and offering thoughtful responses and encouragement.
12. Diverse perspectives are received by open minds, welcoming nods, and sincere compliments, where no thought-filled idea is considered a bad idea as it is initially framed.
13. Not caring who gets the credit, the decisive and encouraging persons on this healthy team become solution providers when methods are defined, decided, declared, and done.
14. Inhibition, and thoughts arising from adverse "No way..." and "Yeah, but..." comments are replaced with enthusiastic and clearly expressed desires to try, if it can be shown that the efforts could make positive and rewarding differences and that the results would be favorable, exceeding expectations.
15. Considerations of reasonable risk are treated as opportunities that may produce viable options.

Healthy perspective discussions promote positive interaction and energizing exchanges of ideas coming from solid ideals. A great core team so involved is acting on the basis of relationships (decisions in support of each other's successes) and cooperative functions (the proof of the relationship's positive character, seen in demonstrated actions) in combination.

Sharing differing views will not alter the essential character of the object or action to be considered. A process of discovery may certainly cause truer "do's" to be formulated when contemplated actions have been weighed carefully and, in balance, are found to constitute best choices.

Submission, Sacrifice, and Service

Three elements of attitude and activity alignment are needed in welcoming diverse perspectives. These are submission, sacrifice, and service. In concert, they represent characteristics of healthy teams who want to grow through open communication and progressive productivity. Look at these three carefully:

1. **Submission** is the willful decision and its declaration to become obedient to shared core values. Because prior agreement on values has been ratified by the core team membership, the members demonstrate that their values will be upheld. They will use them as guideposts of engagement and as evaluation markers of success or failure.

> *Question for your team: What are your core team's shared values and value system to which you and other team participants wholeheartedly submit?*

2. **Sacrifice** is the intentional giving up of that which would otherwise impede progress. Sacrifice shows less interest in self-preservation and more in true investment and service reproduction. Barricades to

success are dismantled for the good of the people and the endeavor. These barricades include over-inflated egos, self-protectionism, excessive control, attitudes of superiority, covert agendas, behind the back negative and destructive conversations, unfavorable intimations, whining, and blatantly offensive behaviors.

Question for your team: How often does your team willingly demonstrate true sacrifice on behalf of the membership and the customers the team serves?

3. **Service** is value-demonstrating provision that consistently seeks the receiver's best interest. It positions and completes actions to assure that the products delivered are qualitatively above what is expected. It freely gives. Service is the outward flow, the natural result, of proper submission to values and the intentional sacrifice of negative elements, willingly replacing them with purposeful action born of agreement on what is right and good.

Question for your team: How does your team know within real life examples that service provision is working well?

The A-B-C's of Constructive Engagement

Constructive engagement on a team doesn't just happen. It is usually positioned by design. In open environments where fresh innovation is bursting from values-driven and creative minds, a great team may need to employ the A-B-C's of interaction to assure that good and proper evaluation is being conducted — that people and their ideas are honored, and appropriate and right conclusions are reached because due diligence has been applied.

The "A" stands for *Affirm the people and obtain the facts*. When new ideas take center stage, appreciate the person and his or her contributions while beginning the process of discovery.

The "B" stands for *Back up to see the bigger picture*. Observe the whole from a broadened perspective. This larger outlook is needed more often than not. Creative genius may need to be assessed from a distance much in the same sense that viewing a magnificent painting may need to be done far enough away to enable the viewer to see and assimilate the whole design.

"B" must always be followed by "C." The third letter stands for *Create a solution in a timeline*. Calendared action is the child of thoughtful deliberation if an exchange is to be more than mere conversation.

The A-B-C process of constructive engagement is a place where original ideas are constructed out of proper evaluations. Plans become the results of sifting information in open environments. This kind of cooperative communication is a common trait of a healthy core team.

In the flowchart below notice that the A-B-C process consists of obtaining the facts, interchanging and weighing ideas, and sifting and distilling them. Decisions come from thorough deliberation of needs and the actions they require. These sequential activities are essential to constructive engagement.

Remove acquiring the facts and the team has little substance to consider. Avoid affirmation and, while there may be discussion, relationships can suffer if courtesy is not present. Replace backing up with movement devoid of clear motives, and clarity is thwarted. Fail to create measurable solutions and actions won't occur. A team so improperly engaged has wasted its time doing nothing more than talking.

The A-B-C process is simple to understand and easy to implement for people who agree on its importance. On a healthy team the process is utilized regularly.

Questions for your team: How often do you participate in constructive engagement? If not often enough, when will you plan on instituting the A-B-C's in your perspective discussions?

A core team who wants to grow will desire better methods of inviting, and learning from, varied perspectives. In addition to the sample questions in the text box above, perhaps your team should consider these:

1. How willing is your team to entertain fresh perspectives?
2. How often should you and your co-workers engage in perspective-sharing discussions and activities?
3. What atmospheres and enhancements would or could make these moments more enlivened and productive?
4. How possible is implementation of fresh views when a new course of action, born of free and open discussion coming from varied perspectives, is considered?
5. What values anchor your team's perspectives, to help ensure that what is presented aligns with what the team has ratified as true and worthy of consideration? Or, put another way, how tied are innovative perspectives and presentations to the inherent principles that form the DNA of your team, its people, and production?
6. If perspective-sharing, as a part of creative problem-solving, is not currently practiced, what are the steps you and your team will take to initiate this important activity?
7. When will you start?
8. To whom will you present your ideas and action plans?

Opportunities to see business challenges and choices through new or renewed views are present when committed people gather to discuss issues and create resolute actions. While resting solidly on principles that shall not change, the core team who wants to develop its people and product, in that order, desires, decides, originates and fulfills freshly formed ideas in creative discussion. Open dialogue characterizes these interchanges. These environments promote freedom of expression and encouragement to participate. These workplaces engender and earnestly seek varying perspectives as part of vital decision-making.

If you serve on a team like this, enhance it. If you don't, endeavor to chance it.

The A-B-C's of Constructive Engagement Flowchart

First: <u>Obtain the Facts</u>, then <u>Begin your interaction</u>.

<u>**A**ffirm</u>

<u>**B**ack Up</u>

<u>**C**reate a Solution</u>

<u>Repeat this cycle</u>.

This process helps sift and distill information and can assist you and your team to choose the best and wisest course of action.

Your best alternative always begins with an informed choice and culminates in behavioral change.

Chapter 3:
A Clean Atmosphere Is Made of Fresh Air

The term "claustrophobic" describes a state of severe restriction. Stress and fear permeate a tightened and inhibiting enclosure where frustration compounds discomfiture because movement is prevented. Helplessness and hopelessness accompany this cramped and unwanted domain. Stale and dank smells abound, stifling free breathing. This place is a prison, a dungeon, a cage. Escape becomes the primary objective for anyone unfortunate enough to exist within its walls.

This is not a pretty picture. Unfortunately, environments with some of these characteristics exist far too often in commercial workplaces. While not jails in the traditional sense, these atmospheres are seen as tight, uncomfortable, unbearable, restrained, and confining. Stress is common and growth is discouraged. Quality relationships are rare as workers are ranked far under, or subservient to, their production. Put-downs are rampant. Gossip reigns. Insecurity is the order of the day.

Within these claustrophobic places three insidious elements rule. These are: micromanagement, intimidation, and attention -grabbing.

Great core teams do not exist here.

Rather, maturing groups proactively seek to improve their workplace atmospheres, not content with needless restrictions. They construct advanced and contributory work habitats. They also know the signs to look for that say that a workplace may not be all it could be. When the signs point to dysfunction, the team addresses and corrects the negatives that could cause unhealthy confinement.

Great core teams become aware of the people who don't fit the productive core team model and the destruction they can create if left to their own devices. Negative contributors are revealed when values are not shared, and when disagreements in vision, lack of excellence in mission, and wrong messages become known. Core teams recognize these square pegs in round holes through the relational and functional stresses they cause. Maturing teams handle these individuals wisely.

Inhibiting persons and their inherent conditions are uncovered for what they really are—the soured airs of the office or field. When they are identified, a process of dealing with them must be constructed from desires to build something better. The idea is to help people and processes improve, showing desired alternatives in attitudes and actions, encouraging progress through truth-telling in atmospheres of genuine care.

Consider the people who micromanage, intimidate, and excessively grab attention. These people may not understand the disruption they cause. Then again, they may.

Pause a moment and reflect on the people whom you have led, or on those who have led you, who personified less than satisfactory attributes, who produced or contributed to stress-filled atmospheres. Can you remember who they were and what environments they fostered? Likely these may be memories you would like to forget, yet learning from them may be important.

How many people were affected negatively or to what degree by dysfunctions of micromanagers, intimidators, and attention-grabbers in work environments with which you have been acquainted? Or, looking at your current condition, who are these people and what effects are they producing? More to the point, are you one of them?

If it can be shown that you, regardless of position or place, desire a more productive workplace atmosphere, free of useless restriction, undue tensions, and meaningless attention-getting, how would you even begin to accomplish the change? Further, if you wanted to actively stimulate stronger relationships and functional excellence, what alterations would *you* initiate to foster best-placed quality and enhanced practices, where mediocre efforts are replaced with superior endeavors? If you were successful, how would your team know that their working atmospheres were improving? What verifiable hallmarks of success would you and the work cluster celebrate?

Comfortable and energizing work spaces are places where people are honored and excellence of provision is achieved not by chance but by choice of a changed design. Change can be uncomfortable no matter the source. Everyone in a work cluster is affected within environments where participants who really want positive change strive to make it happen—especially when that change is unalterably tied to values, vision, mission, and message.

The traits and trends of closed environments, when contrasted with the positive characteristics of contributory atmospheres, become poignant tell-tale signs of whether your work surroundings are beneficial to the people and their production. In unsatisfactory and unsatisfying positions, listen to the people who want to be part of initiating positive change. Determine with them how much they want it and how to make it happen.

Honest discovery shows you that if your team desires positive change, then your team will be the authors and finishers of making the work environments better. The process is not easy but, within a rightful purpose, it is worth the expenditure of efforts to achieve the uplifting goals. The process means confronting negatives with positives in productive atmospheres, telling the truth, living as models of what is desired, correcting error, and congratulating great outcomes.

Let's face it—people choose the atmospheres they bring to work. Responsible people know the importance of their choices, not only for their welfare, but for the wellbeing of the others with whom they work.

When a team member allows or fosters negative emotions then the air becomes polluted quickly and restrictions begin. If this claustrophobic smog is not abated, it can be negatively infectious in profoundly destructive ways.

Three types of individuals contribute to negativity on a team. Their actions in style and substance are detrimental to co-workers; their attributes engender stress-filled and confining work environments. These stifling persons are the micromanager, the intimidator, and the attention-grabber. Let's look at each.

Honest discovery shows you that if your team desires positive change, then your team will be the authors and finishers of making the work environments better.

The Micromanager

The micromanager is an individual who simply doesn't trust other people on the team — either relationally or functionally. Where the term "relationship" is defined as the decision one makes about another's success, the micromanager repeatedly decides that the risk of instilling confidence or sharing competence is too great. Constructive relationships are, therefore, avoided. Because of perceived or real loss of control, this individual wades into and through endless functional details to make sure that processes are going exclusively his or her way, whether or not relationships are hurt.

To this leader or supervisor it appears preferable to promote another person's frustration or failure by discouraging or preventing growth, standing in the way of innovative exploration, limiting education, hindering continued learning, or holding back career advancement. In this insecure state the development of the individual is a threat because, should wins occur, the micromanager may not share in the accolades of success. This unstable working environment is one where function (defined as tasks that demonstrate relationship) proclaims that lack of trust is prevalent and breeds destructive by-products.

Micromanaging inhibits innovation and responsible ownership, pushing an agenda that says "Why try?" to the managed. A typical behavioral pattern shows numerous times when tasks are taken back by the assigner. The insecure manager controls atmospheres and actions so that the owner of the task is constricted in motive and motion, falsely illustrating that no good deed can be done without interference and unwelcome invasion.

Even if an assignee tries to own responsibility of getting jobs accomplished, the credit for success may not be shared or affirmed. Or, if failure is the result, fault-finding can quickly become another reason for generating even greater interference within parties who might otherwise complete each other, if they were allowed to own their tasks well.

Micromanagers set unreasonable expectations for co-workers or subordinates. They foster environments where needless re-entering of process, pushing untimely agendas, promoting unhealthy competition, and unhinging cooperation becomes routine. Have you seen these actions in your workplace?

A micromanager seizes problems before seeking solutions and denies the person being managed an option to win or lose. A micromanager often withholds necessary success tools. He or she looks for the minute difficulties, amplifies them, and then usually reclaims the job to prove an assignee's insufficiency, whether true or false, and may withhold informing the one who was given the initial responsibility that he or she has been relieved.

A micromanager recoils at open communication, that vital tool of commerce and community that shows that information loops are closed and behaviors are changed for the better. Instead, the micromanager seldom—if ever—communicates openly or expresses belief and assurance to another team member, because this kind of interaction could lower the micromanager's importance.

This small leader's endeavors of constriction scream of heightened insecurity. Non-communicative actions foster even greater distances that have to be invaded all over again—a vicious cycle.

Bottom line, a micromanager engages in control activity because he or she is an insecure authority figure who is afraid of personal failures and believes that if someone else succeeds under his or her watch it will somehow diminish that control. Not a pretty picture—and certainly a state of engagement far from the model of great leadership and cooperative core team function.

Workplace atmospheres created by such ineffective leaders are inhibiting and claustrophobic. They breed discomfort and disconnect for those who are led in these ineffectual ways. Eventually the author of the model — the one who does the micromanaging — is shown to be the greatest loser in the exchange.

Great leaders do not micromanage. Great core teams confront the tendencies for anyone on the team to do so.

Micromanaging is wholly apart from mentoring and investment coaching. There are needs for workers to be managed well, taught effectively, evaluated thoroughly, and congratulated warmly. Leaders who desire to create ownership of responsibility within a group have to become acutely aware of how much proximity or distance is required to promote achievement-oriented growth. They have to know or create suitable lines of demarcation that distinguish necessary invasion with permission from overbearing incursion that constricts development.

Understand the motive of the leader or manager. Where the motive is to produce better people and product regardless of who gets the credit, the leader engages less in micromanaging. A secure leader promotes maturity through mentoring and coaching, teaching the follower how it is done. *A strong leader encourages and assists the follower to become better than the leader in the fulfillment of a task.* (Read that sentence again.)

The weak leader has a different motive. This leader feels an incessant need to invade without permission, or is blind to the effects of his or her destructive engagement. That insecurity promotes lack of stability. The result is restricted, choking, and dirty air. It's not comfortable and it is unwarranted. But it need not remain so.

If you are the leader who micromanages, or the one who is micromanaged, understand that these negative traits can become powerful motivators toward healthy change when desires for improvement say the confrontation is worth the effort. It is for you, whether you micromanage or are the micromanaged, to decide if the engagement of changing behavior will inspire you to clean up your environment.

Let's conclude that you have been a micromanager and want to offer your followers an improved atmosphere of trust and confidence, originating from you. How could you do it? Consider these actions:

1. Identify your tendencies toward micromanaging. Recognize the stifled conditions that may exist on your team to which your leadership managing style has contributed. (Don't even look at the rest of these ideas until you have agreed to do this one, first.)

2. Tell your followers that you own responsibility for not managing them as well as you should, that you desire change within yourself for their benefit. Explain that perfection isn't the goal – perseverance is – and that you will lead them on a different level where your model is open to inspection.

3. Define for your followers your new leadership choice, not characterized by micromanagement. Use this list of actions as a discussion tool if it will help. Tell your people that you own responsibility for your actions, that holding you accountable is not their responsibility. Further, explain that you will look to provide a model of leadership that is investment-oriented, showing your people what you want by what you say and do.

4. Look at the people who have been most affected by your style of micromanagement leadership. Identify activities of their job performance that truthfully require less of your presence. List these actions and discuss them with your followers, deciding and declaring that you will invade less in areas where it can be demonstrated that results will not need intrusive influence.

5. Realistically weigh your motives. Why do you think you micromanage? Consider how important control is to you and why it is important. If it can be shown that less control would equate to as-good-as or better-than results from others under your influence, ask yourself if you would be willing to concede this and agree to less hands-on manipulation.

6. Weigh the long-term results of your treatment of those who look to you for leadership. If you don't promote growth, whose development is adversely affected? The truthful answer over time is you, primarily, as well as those you lead.

7. Foster a fresh environment of trust and sharing at work. Start with a new attitude you generate.

8. Make deliberate choices that have the welfare of others at the core of your decisions. Replace your insecurity with a whole new focus on benefiting others. This new view will strengthen you.

9. Decide that you do not want your current insecurity to become the impurity that describes your legacy when all is said and done. If your desire for good is stronger than protecting your position and place, then you will choose to grow your people by entrusting them with more opportunity and responsibility. You will clearly articulate and evaluate courses of action to promote healthy cooperation, ones that you design with them, replacing improper imposition with shared ownership that comes from inclusion.

10. Create environments of open communication. Open lines of communication are defined on **pages 100 - 103 of** *Leadership Is —*. Work within this truth: Communication has not occurred to its most desirable degree until behaviors change. Change your behavior first, recognizing that when a micromanager wants to change, then participation in open communication is not an option between leader and follower, a teacher and student, and the originator sets the pace.

11. Be eager to evaluate your growth and the growth of others whom you lead. Use the **Position Account and Contribution Evaluation (PACE) form found in** *Industrial Strength Solutions* **on pages 315 - 335.**

Evaluation in honesty-driven atmospheres clears the air of the impurity of selfishness and the germs coming from excessive control.

12. Humble yourself. Perhaps this action should precede the others. Humility paves the way for promoting those you lead because a primary self-focus is replaced by a desire to help others win. Your dedication to humility will disengage your tendency to micromanage. The two cannot exist at the same time.

A secure leader promotes maturity through mentoring and coaching, teaching the follower how it is done. A strong leader encourages and assists the follower to become better than the leader in the fulfillment of a task.

If you are the follower who has been micromanaged, consider whether or not the leader who has led you in this style has had cause for his or her invasive activities. Can part of the reason for intrusion be traced to your actions?

While you don't take responsibility for the styles of leadership of the one for whom you work, you do own personal actions that may contribute to perceived or real needs for hands-on management in ways you may not prefer. If you have been micromanaged and, with your leader, want to positively change this working environment, then consider what alterations in your behavior you should take that will contribute to heightened ownership on your part and engender far less need for close scrutiny on your leader's part.

Evaluate your actions with these questions and the answers you provide to them:

1. What would your response be to your leader when he or she changes a management style to foster more responsibility on the part of your core team's members?

2. What attitudes of receptivity or refusal characterize your reactions when a task is given to you?

3. Do you complete the jobs that you have been assigned to you in a faithful manner: on time, on target, and on treasure?

4. How important are closing communication loops to you? What is your definition in practical terms of what communication closure is? How would you define your responsibilities to close the loops on your core team?

5. To whom should you report your fulfillment of tasks, how often, and in what format? Who should initiate the design of the reporting systems you will use?

6. How much do you expect your leader to check up on you? Is checking up on you his or her responsibility and, if so, why?

7. How much initiative do you want to take in task fulfillment?

8. What are the tell-tale signs that you don't require micromanaging controls?

9. If excellence is a goal, then how do others — leaders and co-workers — know you are achieving it?

10. How willing are you to offer help to someone — regardless of status, title, or position — who may not be performing his or her jobs as well as you think they should?

11. How often does your provision and encouragement replace complaining and gossiping?

12. To what degree do your co-workers see you as responsible and inter-dependent with the other members of the core team, knowing you will accomplish your assignments with excellence?

Leadership Is — ,
Industrial Strength Solutions, and *Core Teams Work*
can be ordered at
www.CreativeTeamPublishing.com

Micromanagers and the ones they lead can change a working atmosphere if they want to. As with most healthy changes, the desire to alter behavior for the better is the initial key to unlock the door of responsible ownership.

The interlocking processes and effects that are germane to development of less micromanaging may not be easy to engage, but they are worthwhile nonetheless if the parties involved want cleaner air and the environments of living and contributing the fresh air provides.

If the desire for a better working space includes diminished or eradicated micromanaging, then the parties who formerly participated in miniature leadership will greatly desire superior interaction, where responsible activity replaces the vacuum of excessive control. How much do you and your team want this?

Deliveries and the Kid Who Always Came Through

It was a part-time product delivery job in the 1960s for a high school kid named Ed. Even though his father owned the company, its operations were new to this young man. But Ed needed a summer job, and he accepted the challenge of learning the trade and providing the service.

His daily task was to fill local customer orders at the warehouse, load product onto a company vehicle, and then follow one of several routes to deliver the wares to retail outlets. The hope was that reduced costs of providing this delivery service, along with supplying more immediate responses to customer order needs, would become wins for the company, the kid, and the clientele.

The formula worked as the mileage mounted. Customers were pleased and told the owner. Salesmen promised quicker order fulfillment, and it happened. Customer confidence increased as deadlines for product delivery dates were kept or beat. This was a refreshing combination of customer and satisfaction touch that raised the bars of excellence. Ed, the young delivery boy, put about 80 miles a day on the company vehicle, five days a week, during the summer, without air conditioning! It was hard work, and while the summer job was not prestigious, nor the highest paying position he would ever have, he saw a lot of customers, delivered thousands of cases of products, and made a lot of friends.

Over the course of a few short weeks the owner, warehouse manager, sales manager, salesmen, office administrator, and hundreds of customers became convinced they could count on this delivery kid. When the summer concluded it wasn't hard to imagine why sales and profits had mounted during this time along with the satisfaction of jobs well done. There was no secret as to why there were happier people all the way around. In fact, there really wasn't anything about this arrangement that hadn't worked for multiple benefits.

This was a well-rounded and successful venture. Deliveries by a kid who was on his own, who made personal contact and demonstrated faithfulness, were actions early in a model of customer service that bore fruit then and on many occasions afterwards. Isn't this the way it is supposed to work?

Indeed, it is. When right decisions come from full agreements on best principles, then the practices illustrate that provision with excellence comes from improved atmospheres and maturing people. Micromanaging will not exist here.

The Intimidator

Second on the list of working environment polluters is the intimidator. The intimidator is known by the people he or she offends. This erring person portrays the exact opposite characteristics of a relationship-driven team participant.

Rarely, if ever, does a truly gracious person, firmly established within his or her internal constitution, resort to undue negative influence to get his or her way. Outward trappings and game-playing are less meaningful or perhaps unimportant to a person not caged within aloneness and aloofness. But isolated and distrusting individuals, who do not operate within values of gratitude, encouragement, or team-building, actively employ divisive and destructive tools of interaction. These consist of put-downs, caustic treatment, rudeness, and argumentation, and they are part of a category of a manipulative activity called intimidation.

The intimidator is easy to spot because, like a leopard, the spots on the outside are pretty easy to see. In working relationships the marks of character evidence themselves in chosen attitudes, language, and deeds.

While it is true that blatant blemishes of character dysfunction can be erased and replaced with something far better (unlike the leopard's spots which don't come off) the process of purging an intimidator's character flaws is tough. It's hard because dealing with chronic need for character change may not be readily accepted from outside sources by the one who practices intimidation. Too often an intimidator's defense postures prevent reception of truth. When truth is refused, corrective action is delayed or denied.

To become better, an intimidator must see a need for change and change from the inside, first. Replacing tendencies of put-downs with encouragements to build up is a character adjustment composed within the individual who truly wants to alter behavior because he or she can see the benefits of the transaction. Usually the only way an intimidator will recognize a need for substantive change is by listening to a caring individual who is bold enough to tell the truth to him or her.

Intentionally substituting a primary focus of self-exaggeration with desires to mature and contribute to other people's success, through generosity and gratitude, only comes about where the one with the flaws views a more viable cause and decides that improvement is preferred. That cause, of course, is serving others before serving self. When put into action, that purpose endows a workplace with cleansed air and invigorated breathing. Smiles follow, too.

The one who longs for contribution to other people's successes repositions his or her views of life and works from expanded, expended, and productive perspectives. This person centers on other people—first—and then on what they produce.

A gracious spirit is exemplified from one who is humble enough to recognize and embrace a need for maturity. Exercising graciousness is an action of grace-filled and wholesomely strong character, and it originates from truly thankful people. Gratitude and intimidation are foreign to each other.

The bottom line is this: Intimidating attitudes and acts of thanksgiving simply cannot dwell in the same place at the same time. Changing from selfish superiority to thankful encouragement is a 180 degree alternative for the intimidator who wants to become an authentic and courageous life giver.

Frank's Story

He was a complicated man. Raised in a family where his real father's negative spirit dominated interpersonal interactions with his mother and siblings, Frank's model of home life until his early teenage years was one of put-downs, biting innuendo, excessive criticism, and verbal abuse. At one point, while still a young teen, he considered running away. Later, approaching age 18, he considered the military.

He didn't choose either. However, by the time he reached twenty-one he had earned a reputation with friends or acquaintances as a hard and difficult-to-like person, a cold, calculating, distrusting, and short-tempered man, but one who commanded respect because he had the knack of making money. Actually, he was really good at it. He possessed innate business insight and he used it for all it was worth.

His father died suddenly when Frank was twenty-three, and Frank inherited substantial holdings. He put this seed money to immediate use. By the time his college term concluded, having earned his degree in business, he had amassed quite a sum and employed twenty people in two separate service companies.

Frank was successful, an intelligent man, but he was not wise. The passage of time did not automatically imbue him with vital personal skills that looked beyond treating people from a utilitarian point of view. He was often heard to say that people were only valuable if and when they could help him grow his businesses.

The "make-it-on-your-own" profit-driven business culture he cultivated around him may have been one of the products of a home environment where even the ones who were supposed to be close were put at arm's length. He carried this profit-driven culture over into his own family's life. The woman he married saw she could be well-off if his enterprising business successes continued, but she concluded soon after the "I do" that the income in the bank would be far more important to Frank than his family at home.

Rough and somewhat crude in the treatment of his wife, some of the more awkward moments he used to enjoy were those where he embarrassed her in public. At first she dolefully and quietly seemed to take it, but even this strong lady reached her limit of endurance. Financial security notwithstanding, their marriage lasted five years. It cost him a lot when it dissolved—in money and meaning. But no matter, he figured he didn't need the burden anyway and that he could make his life work without her. He simply plowed on ahead within an expanding vacuum void of significant relationships.

Friendships came and went, none lasted long. Several were defined as "business partnerships." Many of these partners tried to be close because, at first glance, the proximity appeared to be beneficial. But the tighter the connection, the more distance was desired. Getting too near to Frank proved uncomfortable.

The extent of this wealthy man's interest in people was only in what they could produce for him when a project brought them together. As their respective tasks concluded, partners would either hastily remove themselves or simply be discarded. Few of these relationships ended amicably. There was little need above and beyond Frank's greed.

This unhappy and isolated man positioned his accumulation of wealth as his claim to fame. His selfish superiority was seen in outward trappings, of course. But more importantly, it permeated his interactions with other people who were not business partners. Staff members, customers, and vendors were identical to this self-absorbed man. These people were his tools, merely means to his ends.

Frank was lonely. His isolationism was the product of his treatment of others. His two children, a boy and a girl, had stayed with their mother from infancy, following the divorce. In their teenage years they ostracized their father. While at times Frank had tried to win their attentions by showering them with expensive gifts, they required much more than his money and what it bought. They needed a dad. Deep down what they wanted was his heart, not just his hand.

As these young people grew, married, and birthed families of their own, they would occasionally try to talk to their dad about bridging the distance they all knew existed.

After repeated efforts they became convinced he was not listening. In their maturing years they wondered if he was capable of a fundamental character change—a spot-cleansing they knew could only come from within him.

As Frank advanced in years, but not in maturity, he began to witness his circle of peers, both in age and acquisition, start to shrink. Some died in their fifties and, with his kids out on their own, intense solitude became the norm for this disgruntled individual. It was all "I" for Frank, and it had been this way for most of his life of sixty-two years.

He passed away just before his sixty-third birthday. A few acquaintances and family attended his memorial, but most preferred to remain aloof. There was little to recall and less to honor. You see, many years had passed since the conclusions of their partnerships, and most of his family had been kept at arm's length. He had lived and died alone.

The heart of intimidation is the decision to judge people as objects or object lessons rather than as special opportunities for investment and apprenticeship. To the intimidator, networks are profit centers and people are producers.

Atmospheres where intimidation is practiced are conditions of closed-off relationships. They are black holes where conversation is sucked away and freedom and creativity are drained. Vital open discourse, genuine encouragement, heart-felt affirmation, and hearty celebrations are squelched or prevented.

The "I" of Intimidation represents Isolation. The person who intimidates validates aloofness and is unwilling to risk cultivating relationships. If letting down a guard and exercising humility are necessary actions to make and keep friends, then the intimidator relinquishes these in favor of more surface convenience put-offs or demoralizations of others, with the goal of making him or herself most important.

Intimidation wells up from an unsure and self-deprecating person. When this character flaw is identified and confronted, then the interaction will often produce elevated defensiveness, anger, or maybe even rage. For Frank it was far easier to showcase childish antics than it was for him to humbly reach out to others, whether for his or their benefits. In fact, that reaching, were it to have occurred, would have engendered virtually instantaneous reconsideration of the rules of engagement with nearly everyone in association with him. In other words, he would largely have been greeted with openness. His life probably could have been more meaningful. However, he was too far removed from the warmth of humanity to bridge the chasm of severed relations. Apart from his children, most of the others in his life forgot or refused. They relegated his intimidation to the ash heap of dysfunctional relationships — because those are what it had created.

If you work with an intimidator there are several maxims that, when employed, can help you endure, persevere, and perhaps model behaviors that may cause the intimidating person to gaze into a mirror of self-reflection, if he or she is open enough. Changing revealed character may be a long and wearisome process, but whether you succeed or not, you will truly grow as you contribute, and the results may just surprise you. You will appreciate the efforts you make to improve the work environment and the people in it because you seek the best and are acting on your desires for improvement. Do these:

1. Give your best, regardless. Your character should stand as positive and uplifting, whether or not your leader cares. This is a tough call, but it is also a touch call—your touch can pierce the false walls of put-downs and needless criticisms, and replace them with genuine interest.

2. Tell the truth. Intimidation thrives on innuendo, half-truth, or no truth. Assure you have the facts relating to a topic of business and speak them plainly. Where you know the veracity of your comments, stick to them unreservedly.

3. Avoid imputing or impugning motive of your intimidating leader. Let the discovery of motive be their journey, not yours. Your responsibility is to observe action, and collect and present facts in a non-emotionally-driven, neutral environment. Don't get rattled. Be yourself and be staunchly committed to the endurance of telling the truth and operating within it.

4. Be upfront. Talking about an intimidator behind his or her back to others who may have experienced the same unfortunate treatment is self-defeating and self-deprecating, not to mention that this gossip

undermines your credibility. If you possess the opportunity or the level of trust required to assist the intimidator in changing his or her ways for the better, let it be known and shown that you are a person of upfront confidence born in confidentiality, not prone or party to behind-the-back destructive conversations.

5. Treat accusations and put-downs as non-life-threatening. Whenever possible, take them in stride. Where criticisms are unfounded, let them roll off. If confrontation is required to right a wrong, calmly, assertively, and with assurance tell the truth to the people who need to hear it. Your job's role may be tried and tested by your character in difficult times. Your life's road may take you into many situations where, because you refuse to allow intimidation to control you, you will still present best practices during the fray and be better for it at the end of the day. Do your jobs well, no matter the circumstances, because of your strength of character. Your contributions within the challenges will outlive the negatives, and may outline the courses for greater moments of goodness and excellent production because they are based on higher morals.

6. Where criticisms coming from the intimidator are based on mistakes you've made, corrective actions you need to take, or processes you should improve, humble yourself to receive truth regardless of the attitude of the one telling it, and then do the right and best things. Improve your attitude and aptitude.

Correct and realign because you desire to be a responsible party in the exchange. You and your team will mature as a result.

7. Strive to be the best product producer you can be. Realize that intimidators usually have only one evaluation grid through which they weigh people's effectiveness and that grid is "what the actions of the other person do for me." Regardless of that grid, contribute well because *you* desire faithfulness to be a hallmark and proof point of your solid character, demonstrated faithfully to even an unworthy leader. You will be the better man or woman because of it.

8. Model what you want. This is one of the **"Twelve Laws of Understanding" from** *Leadership Is —*. **See Chapter 7, "Creating Leadership Models that Work" beginning on page 145, and on page 207 of** *Core Teams Work*. These laws are written for those who want to live in a viable value system. Anyone who employs them becomes a leader in principle and practice. Through conscientiously applying the laws, the person who wishes to create and live in best practices will create a model that an insecure leader, if he or she practices intimidation, will begin to notice whether or not a "changing of the spots" of that leader's character occurs.

9. Position healthy distance between you and the intimidating and over-bearing person so you can contribute holistically for as long as possible. There are times when exiting will be the best course. If,

however, exiting is shown not to be the most advantageous move, then back up in your dealings with the bullying person to see the clearest picture and, with accurate information and neutral emotion, tell the truth and stand firm when the necessary interactions do occur. Discipline is required in difficult interchanges and will inspire your actions to develop contributory relationships. Your good works will inspire those around you who are or may become the next onslaught targets for the character-inept and intimidating leader. Through your example you will help others endure and engage appropriately.

10. Forgive. This action is absolutely the most powerful tool you or anyone else possesses, so use it. It doesn't matter if the lording and pretentious supervisor or manager (no matter the title) never requests it — grant it anyway. Forgive the offender and forgive yourself at the same time where you have allowed your own negativity to creep in or bear unwelcome fruit in exchanges with the intimidator. Forgiveness is the decision to no longer hold to account an action of another or yourself. In other words, while the difficulty or offense may be remembered, the penalty is either considered paid or erased altogether.

It's one thing to know how to handle the intimidator — it's another if you're it. So let's consider changing the spots on the leopard.

If you are one who has utilized intimidation you may be able to convince yourself that you should alter your perspective and change your action. If this is even a remote consideration, then you must decide what steps you will take to begin this important life-change journey that may, at its conclusion, prove to be one of the most desirable and positive decisions you have ever made.

Eradicating negatives from character is not an easy accomplishment. The actions involved are much more than items to check on a list of "To Do's." However, you can start to make and fulfill commitments for desired and improved behaviors. Practice what you want to portray—a life and its leadership apart from intimidation. Engage in this exchange—trade the old for new. You will mature and help your people grow even as you do.

If you truly seek to treat people, regardless of your position or theirs, from a non-intimidating posture, the good news is that you will positively impact the atmosphere that surrounds you and the people with whom you interact. You will breathe fresh air into your work environment. This newness will be welcomed by those who look to you for team-building examples, those that endure and mature. In fact, it will appear to be a whole new day, because it is.

Here are some of the vital steps you can take:

1. Identify your intimidation tendencies and habits. Admit that you exercise these. You may request a trusted co-worker for a personal assessment, assuring the person that when the truth is presented you will not return a judgment toll or practice recrimination. If you have developed the reputation, rightly earned or not, of getting back at people who disagree with you

after they've told you things you may not enjoy hearing, then make absolutely sure you let the truth-teller know that he or she will not be judged for their perceptions as they fulfill your assessment request.

2. Adopt a truly open attitude. One of the marks of this desired character trait is effective listening. Pay attention to content without prematurely reaching a conclusion. An active and respect-filled engagement of receiving truth is a measure of developing maturity.

3. Where it can be shown that you have offended others, be person enough to apologize with sincerity. In other words, mean it, don't just mouth it. You may have to come down a notch or two, or three, or more — but you will be better for it as will the person to whom the apology is addressed. If this kind of action is foreign, then give it a passport to a new freedom of expression for you and your core team. Apologizing, and its attending result of genuine forgiveness, is a cleansing activity granted and received by both parties when embraced fully. The exchange is life-altering, for the better. You may add years to your life; regardless, you surely will add life to your years.

4. Don't hide. Covering up or refusing to talk about your responsibilities is not part of restitution. Openness shows you are sincere about change. If you have created impure air that has shortened the breaths and contributed to the deaths of people's value and positive function in your organization, then

take the stand you should take — admit, confess, make better decisions, and move up. Because you are more important than the mistakes you've made, let the goals of building stronger relationships (the positive decisions you make about other people's successes) become new motivators toward improved actions within your networks.

5. Silence the negative voices — the ones in your mind that say intimidation is a good course. You know those voices and where they come from. They are the ones who grant the supposed license to put someone else down. They are the negative encouragers that implore you to demean a subordinate, even if in misguided judgment you think you are doing it for their benefit. Most often the push to put someone else down and the self-argument that discrediting another person is right because they deserve it, represent lying propositions. You know it and so do others. If you are the intimidator, consider that the main motive of intimidation is the desire to deprecate another in the hopes of heightening your stance and increasing your power. It's a false premise. It's shifting sand. It is known to be untrue because it doesn't last — ever. Squelch the demons that encourage you to engage in intimidation. Conquer these serpentine voices and insidious influences, or they will continue to conquer you.

6. Seek a larger view, a fresh perspective that honors people as people instead of objects of convenience.

Cease rushing to conclusions with the intent to identify fault where, according to assessments born of a demeaning spirit, someone must take the blame. Of course, there are times when the cause of a dysfunction must be discovered. Of course, there are moments when corrective actions are necessary. What is referenced here is the covert, perhaps overt tendency, regardless of the degree of a mistake, for intimidation to revel in the chance to degrade a fellow worker or team member. Instead of doing this, take the higher road. Become the growing and maturing person who treats people well, regardless. Become a student of improved methods of personal engagement, sincerely wanting the best for your followers and associates. Teach those you influence a better way because you have chosen it for yourself.

7. Balance critique with congratulations. This mindset is important. It requires the reserves to do it often. The mindset comes from your decision about another's success. The reserves come from the responsible affirmations you have offered as part of working together. It is these reserves on which you draw when you need to critique. In other words, if you have to criticize, do it from the foundation of a trusted relationship. These transactions develop both your character and your followers' characters and improve your performance and theirs, simultaneously.

8. Seize the positive before grabbing the negative. Actively look for ways to help an employee or co-worker win. Acclaiming works better than profaning.

9. Accept praise for your improved behavioral adjustments because you will have rightfully earned it. When you make the decision to become a person of quality leadership who wants the best for yourself and those you impact, you will find yourself sacrificing for those who follow you. Your actions will not go unnoticed; in fact, they will mark you as one whose practices validate your principles. When people tell you that you are accomplishing greater works, accept the accolades with grace, humility, and heart-felt thanks.

10. Utilize tools to remind you of important and life-changing decisions you are making, or have made. These tools can take many forms. A calendar or journal may be one to help you plan and remember. When you make life-altering commitments that help others win, including yourself, remember the dates of your choices. These may be more important in significance than your birthday or anniversary if they provide the stimulus that produces a better person who no longer intimidates others. Other tools may be re-reading a book that helped you frame a momentous decision, talking with a friend, spouse, or counselor whose presence and contributions are supportive, hearing a song again that you associate with life change, going to a special place that you

remember as set apart because of the decisions you made there ... you get the idea. The key is to identify the tools and engage them. Let the tools motivate you to continue down the good paths you are considering or have chosen.

11. Associate with others whom you admire, who do not intimidate people to build themselves up. Listen to what they know. Learn from the learned. Grow from the mature and positive individuals — don't wallow in the manure of the negative ones. Be mentored by those who are uplifting and successful for the right reasons.

12. Invest. Become a mentor, be accountable to yourself, and show accountability to others. Teach what you are learning and living. *Leadership Is —*, **pages 73-76,** describe the positional placement of authority and accountability for every person on a great team, especially one in proper alignment with leadership that builds legacy. On most teams there are people with authority over you, those who share responsibilities at your level (your peers), and those who look to you for leadership. Your opportunity, as one who refuses intimidation and replaces it with investment, is to show the people who observe your improvements how to do the same thing. There may be no better opportunity of building enduring legacy than that of teaching what you have become convinced is right and good. The teacher who models his or her example with excellence will inspire the

students who want to grow. Teach what you know. Your changes of behavior will speak volumes. Those lessons live.

The Attention-Grabber

Third in our list of three atmosphere chokers is the attention-grabber. We've all seen and heard them, experienced their capers, sometimes fallen into spasms of uproarious laughter because their antics were really funny, or rolled our eyes and hoped for a needed respite — soon.

Some people, no matter their position, have to be the center of attention. They think that apart from blatant personal demonstration they could be relegated to the background. In an effort to show us they are *something*, they show off, try to become bigger than life, and exaggerate, often doing so with consequential embarrassment to themselves and others around them. A foolish demonstration most often is born of a fool.

Attention-grabbers can initially be perceived as life-energizers in a group. They may exercise Impact Leadership in the formation of a work cluster or at the outset of an endeavor. **(Please see Chapter 2, "Leadership Tracks and Traits" from *Leadership Is* — for an explanation of Impact, Influence, and Investment Leadership).** Their enthusiasm, playfulness, and outgoing exhibitions of entertainment know no boundaries for any who will listen and participate. Upfront, loud, and sometimes pushy, the attention-grabber seeks to be the center-focus on the team regardless of any person's position, including theirs.

On the surface the attention-grabber may be harmless and prove over time to be innocuous. However, the tendency is to afford more undue notice and reliance on someone who may not prove that they are worthy of that degree of approbation—at least at first. Personality is driven; its characteristics are subject to the choices of behavior exercised by the owner. Therefore, it is important to cut through the foolishness and overt displays of superior confidence to ascertain the presence of vastly more important attributes: faithfulness, commitment, reliability, trust, truth-telling, and fulfillment of roles and responsibilities. No flashes in the pan are allowed when a great team gets down to business. Of course, gregarious personalities are welcomed. Attention-grabbers intermesh well when they know and show self-control. There are good reasons why the class clown is included. Great humor comes naturally to many people who are truly a breath of fresh air on a team. All work and no play, or no humor in the workplace environment, can make a project more arduous than it needs to be and the prospect of its completion downright difficult. Drudgery is as much of an enemy as too much playing when a job needs to be done.

What is really required here, of course, is balance. The attention-grabber can be a gifted contributor to the group's enterprise if there are declarations and proofs of values agreement, vision adherence, mission accomplishment, and life-truth assent. The attention-grabber may be your best sales person, or the pushiest person you've ever known, depending on how he or she chooses to use the expansive and explosive personality traits they possess.

It again boils down to choices of behavior. If your team possesses one of these explosive folks, then be sure to communicate well and often with him or her about the contributions that produce stronger lines of interconnectivity and positive communication. No innuendo, behind-the-back criticisms, or put-downs of the person who is bigger-than-life shall be permitted. When an attention-grabber focuses energies in the right directions, he or she may just become one of the truest contributors to the successes of your team.

Over-analyzing one who demonstrates overtly gregarious traits can become a trend to avoid. Rather, embrace the person and let the proximity of engagement become the proving ground of faithful commitment. In other words, before criticizing or commending, communicate openly, and see what develops.

If you are the attention-grabber, then exercise maturity. Know when to display and when to restrain for the benefit of the group and the commitments your team shares. Don't sacrifice your personality, choose better behaviors.

The key here, for every great team, is to form an alliance of cooperation based on agreed values, vision, mission, and message. When these are in play, people with varying personalities contribute out of their strengths and exercise self-control. In diversity, there is tremendous energy and synergy when essential elements of good character align.

The Leader Who Didn't Measure Up

Matt was a classic explosive character—he just had to be in front of the team, all of the time. At work, in his leadership role, he was good at group interaction and facilitation. People naturally responded to him. He was boisterous, funny, engaging, and larger than life.

But Matt had a problem. His inward character did not line up with his outward demonstrations of jovial and attractive buoyancy. His true nature did not couple with his entertaining and motivating words.

The struggle was seen in his work product or, more accurately put, his lack of commitment to completing a job well and within agreed time frames. Too often he modeled irresponsibility. When he did not meet a deadline or didn't empower his team with necessary tools and leadership, his perennial explanations were that it was his leader's fault, or that the failure belonged to another team member. The list of persons he blamed lengthened as he sought to shift responsibilities from himself.

Matt had been given a position of leadership because his engaging and outgoing personality was seen as a display of confidence. This assessment proved to be unfortunate. Inwardly there were big problems—many of them unearthed over time, when circumstances got tougher and his contributions fell short.

Some of his dysfunctions were discovered to be:

- Promising actions he did not perform or was late in completing

- Consistent needs for his supervisor to follow him, if not chase him down, to assure tasks were being fulfilled
- Poor communication of followed-through action (few even knew what he was doing)
- Blaming others for his issues
- Lack of willingness to accept constructive admonition or instruction on improvement, especially when it meant he had to change
- Demanding more and producing less
- Lack of faithfulness in small items
- Leaving or avoiding meetings where he was not to be the leader or up- front person
- Openly criticizing others in private or public conversations, especially the people who were his supervisors
- Complaining about negative conditions without offering solutions
- Positioning himself as an authority on a subject when he was proven at a subsequent time to not have had sufficient understanding
- Many words and little action
- Personality plus, with little or no personal commitment
- Rarely investing in another team member for that member's benefit

Eventually Matt was moved from his leadership position. In the final analysis his team was gratified that this was done. Many were happy to see him repositioned to another department where he was not in charge.

This attention-grabber had revealed his true colors and they didn't paint a very attractive picture.

True character is revealed in the day-to-day details. Attention-grabbers can be effective contributors if they choose well. You and your team will see evidences of their true constitutions in the actions they choose, especially off the stage.

> In diversity, there is tremendous energy and synergy when essential elements of good character align.

Handling Stress

Many of my office visitors like to use the stress card I have placed on my desk within their reach. You may have seen one of these cards. By simply placing a thumb on the center black square, and by observing the color that remains on the square when the thumb is removed, a person can tell whether or not they are stressed. Now while the test is highly unscientific, a lot of folks try it before launching into our discussions. I suppose that in the lightheartedness of the moment, stress can actually be reduced.

But if stress is a large part of the atmosphere where you work, how do you know its signs and how do you deal with it? What are its origins? Certainly micromanagers, intimidators, and attention-grabbers can be stress-encouragers, but the fault of the presence of a stress-filled room should not be laid at their doorsteps exclusively.

Sometimes stress is simply a part of the job because the job produces it. Forged and forced timelines, shortages of funds, unreliable suppliers, flaky customers, unreasonable expectations, inflation, deflation, lack of supply, loss of contact, unresolved issues, violations of principle, or failures of equipment—the list goes on and on. Other times, stress originates when frustrations replace closure or perspectives are obscured. Stress may come because a team is not cognizant of what is in store within a job requirement, and even if the team becomes aware, the members may still be put into disarray when unwanted circumstances materialize.

"Stress" can be defined in many ways. For the purposes of *Core Teams Work Their Principles and Practices*, consider this definition: Stress is a state of anxiety arising by degrees from inhibitors that frustrate planned experiences or from the accumulation of factors whose appearance or consequences are outside one's control.

Stress can bode stifling environments and permeate a workplace with negatives. It is an unwelcome guest whenever it appears. But stress and its by-products can also act as motivators to change an unfavorable situation into something better.

The ways in which one deals with pressure points are varied, of course. Methods are influenced heavily by personality, experience, education and environment. On a healthy core team, strains can be handled best where a team's values, vision, mission, and message become prevailing, central, and solidifying truths, no matter what.

Here are some ideas:

1. Take a breath in the heat of the moment, especially if the circumstances are overpowering, to understand the cause. Find the source of the stress.

2. Back away from the intensity to provide space to think and react more circumspectly. Take a walk (or a run) around the building if you need to. If time and space permit, provide a moment to clear your mind.

3. Remove distractions that would otherwise cloud your vision and hinder your understanding of the focus of your endeavors.

4. Discipline yourself to rest on assurances of who you are, what you are called to do, what your desires are, and who will receive the benefits of your engagement.

5. Take a complete break—a nap or a vacation or something in between. Sometimes simply getting away is the best answer to provide an opportunity for clearer thinking and solution provision.

6. **Talk to a trusted co-worker or leader from a mindset of discovering a workable solution. (Please see Chapters 4, 5, 6, and 7 of *Industrial Strength Solutions*).**

7. Understand that some degree of stress may be part of the job you hold and its functional responsibilities. Use this understanding as an educator to help you engage and eventually rise above or solve it.

8. Recognize that some causes of stress are out of your control. In humility, with strength based on right values, manage those things you can and let the others go.

9. Remember the phrase, "This, too, shall pass." Smile. Equanimity, or mental and emotional balance, is the gift within a person who is assured through faith that the momentary will dim when presented with the permanent.

10. Trust in Higher Authority. Faith in God and the implementation of a value system based on eternal principles will help you endure and mature through points of life that you may not comprehend now.

11. Forgive yourself and others. Guilt-free is a state of being stress-free.

12. Dwell in positives. Choose best attitudes and actions founded on elevating and life-giving truths.

Changing the air where you work is more than hoping it gets purer over time. It won't unless someone takes the initiative to improve the surroundings through direct engagement. Will that person be you? Ask yourself: What part am I willing to play to stimulate, support, and own improvements in the atmosphere where I work? Then ask: When will I start, and how will my co-workers know?

The Purification Grid

Create a working environment of freshened air. Filter what you don't desire through the fine mesh of what you do desire.

Consider using a purification grid. Much like the effects of an air purifier, the result of passing negative particles through positive influence is a revived perspective born of cleansed people and motives. In the core team workplace, fresher air is evidenced when truth, willful allegiance to core values, and freedom to grow compose an energizing atmosphere.

Forcing impure traits through an inter-woven mesh of better relationships and superior functions goes a long way toward solving the appalling messes of many postmodern, negatively-charged environments. Breathing easier is worth the effort, so consider using the grid to rid your work spaces of unwanted particles.

The purification grid is accessible to any organization. The elements that make it up disinfect the impurities that pass through it; in fact, the grid changes whatever it touches. Use it—it's available to you.

The purification grid is made of the team's interlocking and unbending agreements on values, vision, mission, and message which constitute their "Code of Achievement." **(Please see *Leadership Is*— pages 73 - 76 for a full explanation of the Code of Achievement.)** Pass your negatives through these essentials and experience transformation.

- Why does it work? Truth conquers error every time, no matter how long it takes.
- How does it work? When negative attitudes and actions are weighed and evaluated against the relational and functional standards that your team has decided compose their purification grid, attitudes and actions change, or those who desire the negative more than the positive will likely depart.
- Use of the grid is self-evaluating, celebration-encouraging, and correction-simulating. When a team engages the grid, then those who want best deliverables align with it.
- Dedicated core team people who agree on values, vision, mission, and message will replace foul air with fresher atmospheres of resolute strength and increased output because they *want* their relational and functional behaviors to match their "Code of Achievement."

Establishing the standards for operational efficiencies born of relational integrity and agreement on function, the grid's unbendable truths cooperate to produce desired and long-lasting effects when people are truly willing to change. Here are some of the expected results:

1. Helping the micromanager and the micro-managed to improve their behaviors
2. Assisting and encouraging the intimidator to value his or her people more
3. Positioning the attention-grabber to circumspectly review his or her behavioral contributions, to assure

that they match the constitution of the team's greatness

4. Learning how to handle, reduce, or eliminate stress

A clean atmosphere is made of fresh air. Refresh yours. Remember, when atmospheres of existing air are purified, the workplace becomes better.

Stress levels lessen as the lesson of blending values, vision, mission, and message permeates the surroundings. Work toward these beneficial results by filtering negatives through positives. You and everyone around you will breathe easier.

Chapter 4:
Truth and Tenacity

Great leaders and dedicated followers share a commitment to do their jobs well. Quality provision is a result of this commitment. Right people desire the best and contribute from high levels of integrity. These dedicated individuals confront tough issues with truth and face challenges with graceful and enduring strength. Their heartfelt desires for authenticity are seen in their actions, which come from mutual agreements on principle. They persevere with positive attitudes and productive actions born of solid character. Who they are and what they do compose the cooperative elements in the constitution of an effective core team.

Truth works, and truth wins. It is foundational to a successful team. It provides immovable confidence that a course of action is correct because it is based on knowledge that right standing leaves the right people standing, regardless. No matter the force of conflict, source of disappointment or how coarse others may be in the process, truth shines through. Herein is the birth of confidence. Truth is tenacious — it simply won't give up.

Confidence

Confidence is the product of faith anchored firmly on enduring principle. Within a group of people who exude confidence and exclude diffidence there are shared reasons for performing actions based on assurances of what lasts.

Confidence is composed of two core elements. One is *hope*. Hope is a wish or a dream, but it is also more. Here it constitutes a strong and continuing desire for the good, right, and true. Hope that does not disappoint, and is not disappointed, focuses and frames best results that may come to pass if enough diligent effort is put forth.

The second element is *evidence*. This is proof of a result that is sure to come. When right motives and dedicated actions are combined toward fulfillment of a worthwhile endeavor, evidence states that winning will occur. Completion of a goal may reside in the future, but the indication of good outcome is based on confirmed and irrefutable testimony. History proves that enduring and positive results come to pass when correct belief and right action are purposefully aligned and combined.

Confidence interweaves hope and evidence. Assurance of outcomes requires more than wishful thinking—it demands repeatable proofs based on past demonstrations that truth wins. It always has; it forever will.

A great team is confident of beneficial consequence when its actions are immovably anchored on truthful guidelines. Desires based on a lasting foundation cause a team to be tenacious about fulfilling what they know is right, because truth and tenacity are inseparable.

Truth is principle proven over time. Tenacity is the consistent application of enduring principle, seen in words and works. A team perseveres to complete their goals because they are convinced they are correct — their strength and endurance are by-products of their well-placed confidence.

Leaders and followers who possess long-lasting dedication to see a situation through sometimes face odds that must be overcome. They are tenacious to complete a calling, especially when naysayers and ne'er-do-wells offer up negatives, fault-finding, whining, complaining, or worse.

Tenacious people who have confidence based on truth compose a powerful group. Great core teams are made up of people of confidence. Any who desire to be part of a confidence-endowed team encourage and learn from people of this kind of character.

Confidence is a vitalized part of a core team who believes in their people, procedures, and products. Truth and tenacity are the intangible characteristics of a work cluster that is dedicated to more than words alone. On a maturing core team, confidence, truth, and tenacity show commitment toward fulfilling deeds and finishing well, no matter the degree of difficulty encountered along the way.

You may be serving on a team with confident people. You may wish you were. Become more of a person of confidence yourself, and your team may develop into a group of growing individuals who surpass expectations in their relationships and functions because of your example.

If you agree with these ideals and want to see them activated in your group, then take this one step further. If you desire confidence, then you will seek clarity and closure.

Clarity and Closure

"Clarity" is defined as seeing a course of action transparently, without obstruction. Clarity lives when reasons behind actions are known. It is the opposite of confusion where people busily contribute loads of time and energy, but may not understand why.

Great core teams strive for clarity when they embark on worthwhile endeavors. They know that with clarity comes purpose; with purpose, passion; with passion, desire and motivation for excellence; and with excellence, better production, communication, and closure.

Clarity * Purpose * Passion * Desire * Motivation * Excellence * Better Production * Communication * Closure

Clarity is the first choice of a team who is presented with a prospect, challenge, or opportunity. The bigger the job, the greater is the need for understanding on the parts of those who are tasked with its completion. As understanding gives way to purpose, passion is employed to embrace the tasks wholeheartedly and fulfill them well. Clarity *defines* the project and *designs* the procedures.

This isn't to say that everyone on a team must understand every aspect of their team's contributions. It is to say that anyone tasked with a role should understand not only the duty of that particular job, but the value of their engagement.

"Closure" is defined as the responsible conclusion to a process. Closure is the completion of a task and the knowledge of its fulfillment. It is seen in quality accomplishments and the communication of the facts to the people who need to know. Closure *performs* the assignments and *informs* the assigners.

Closure is a method that is too often overlooked or assumed. Great core teams see closure as necessary to finishing well, so they integrate it into their jobs. They comprehend the necessity of not only fulfilling a task with excellence, but also communicating its completion with timeliness.

A great team's work procedures include closing the communication loops. People dedicated to closure do not leave pieces of information dangling, where persons who assigned the tasks are unaware of whether or not the tasks are done. Teams who exercise closure fulfill cycles of communication by sharing news of completion with right people, in right times, and in right ways.

Closure looks at a job's accomplishment and recognizes that while truth and tenacity might have faced sometimes insurmountable odds, at the end of the day a job was completed well, a customer was satisfied, and the right people were told.

So let's put this in proper perspective. A solid core team who possesses and practices agreement on core values, vision, mission, and message will desire, promote, and exercise truth-telling. They will express confidence (faith) in the product's fulfillment, regardless of circumstances. They are assured on the basis of history's lessons of endurance and perseverance that what they are doing is right. They are tenacious in their efforts because they know that truth wins. This team seeks clarity of purpose. They are passionate about fulfilling their responsibilities and closing communication loops when their jobs are over.

Do you want to contribute to, and serve on, a team like this?

It Was Only a Hike

It is said that if you really want to know someone, go camping with them. Perhaps that's true.

The oppressively hot day was half gone when the idea of hiking to the top of a small mountain was presented to the group of fourteen. Reception was favorable at first—the discussion about the assent was conducted in the shade of trees that provided relief from the heat. But as the hike commenced, with parents and several small children in a long line, footsteps soon became labored. Shade devolved into long pockets of bright sunshine and its accompanying rising temperatures. Stirred dust invaded the air and scrub brush scratched bare arms and legs. The trail became pockmarked with stones. Feet slipped, ankles bent. Traversing from rock to rock and constantly ducking to avoid branches sapped energy and drained spirits.

As a midpoint was reached after nearly an hour of panting, pushing, and pulling, everybody felt the strain. Original enthusiasm had long since dimmed. Several adults in the group breathed hints like, "I'm content with this scene, why bother to keep going?" Kids and parents were thirsty. Water was rationed. Tempers shortened as beads of sweat dripped from everyone.

Actually, the midpoint stop was a refreshing respite. A rivulet, whose source appeared to be far up the ravine, flowed near the trail. As water danced over the rocks its peaceful murmurs bid the group to recoup. This shaded intermission provided a rest from the pace, and a relaxing space for casual conversation. The group considered that if there was a place to turn around and go back to camp, this was it.

But everyone knew a trail still beckoned. Sheer perseverance and mounting desire for closure drove some of the group to consider, and then to decide, to go for it—to complete the journey.

When this decision was made, the group ensured that those who wished to return to base camp had provision enough to do so, that children were properly accompanied on the descent, and that all knew the way back. After those who wished to return had departed, the remaining climbers resumed their hike up the mountain. The trail was steeper, narrower, more over-grown and challenging, evidence that far fewer hardy souls had toiled up this way.

But in far less time than the work of the walk indicated would be necessary, the summit of the relatively small mountain was reached. For a moment no one spoke. All in this small team smiled at each other and drank from water bottles and canteens.

They took in the scenery, savoring the sensation. What they viewed all around them was simply breathtaking. The river danced before them, interrupted by beaver's dams. Strong trees graced the water's banks and spoke of endurance and hope. Vines clung tenaciously to soaring boughs and interlaced themselves in a race to ascend the heights. Shade was abundant. Downriver and beyond the dams, eddied waters gathered their strength, joining forces. Emboldened, their flows lunged and plunged toward valleys below.

Eyes strained on distant horizons, relishing endless and lofty landscapes. Spirits lifted. Remembrances of sore backs, weary legs, pouring sweat, and heavy, dusty breaths were replaced by admirations and congratulations. These souls were drawn into the majesty of the mountain and embraced awestruck and intimate moments of wonder. This time and place was beyond compare, and was shared by those who had not settled for the mid-trail's convenient and comfortable surroundings, as refreshing as they had been.

For these companions who had longed for peak experiences, their quests had been achieved through heightened diligence, firm dedication, and hard work. They had cooperated from a core belief that there was more in store if they persevered. They had to know, as they had decided to go, that their expenditures of energy and toil might just prove worth it.

These casual but committed adventurers had pressed on and had won the prize. Exhilarations from the event would remain delightful to recall. Descending the mountain was pure pleasure, as was the telling of the story of the sights and sounds of the experience around the campfire that night.

Truth and tenacity form frameworks of action for the core team that wants to produce the best of which it is capable. Right relationships and motives encourage focused attitudes and methods. Kindred thoughts and minds are brought together through enduring relationships, where reliability and relevance are hallmarks of commitment and the evidence of perseverance. A core team that exercises truth and tenacity produces excellence and exceeds expectations because they desire to be dependable. They are reliable and highly accountable.

Reliability and Accountability

Reliability is a cousin of accountability. They work together. In fact, these two terms are often used as synonyms. But there are differences as intended here. Accountability is repeatable proof over time that a person and his or her performance can be counted upon, that *consistent results* will accompany the process of endeavor.

Reliability, however, describes *reliance* on the *ability* of the person tasked to perform a job. In other words, the degree of competence matches the need of the task's fulfillment.

When truth and tenacity are present, then reliability will be the result if the person and production are aligned correctly. When the person tasked with the job possesses the ability to get it done, in full agreement with, and adherence to, the values, vision, mission, and message of the organization, then the relevant match will firmly attach the person to his or her performance.

Remember that people are more important than what they produce and that production with excellence is the natural result of a prioritized configuration of relationship and function. Reliance on ability, where one's competence is correctly aligned with reasonable expectations, is proven repeatedly as problems are faced with positive attitudes and a solution-thinker's actions produce best-deliverables.

So, to summarize, here is how these concepts and actions come together on a core team in these ways:

1. A project or task is assigned.
2. Confident team members are convinced of the validity of their cause. They are tenacious to complete their endeavors.
3. Clarity assures understanding of reasons behind actions and defines specific goals within reasonable timelines.
4. Right people are tasked with right jobs. Relationships (decisions about another's success) align people best

suited to complete the requirements with appropriate responsibilities.

5. Problems are faced with open communication, truth-telling, and strong perseverance to fulfill responsibility, not letting temporary chance or change dictate wins or losses. Challenges are overcome to secure the prize.

6. People who are committed to excellence demonstrate their understanding of roles and, in fulfilling them, prove reliability. The relevant match of the person to the need builds the individual, completes the project, and produces an end-deliverable that equals or exceeds expectations.

7. Closure lets the team know that when the job is completed, the standards of performance for the task are met or surpassed, and the right people are informed, they've succeeded.

Pains and gains are ebb and flow partners. One exists as a balance to the other as movement toward accomplishment of worthwhile goals is made. Teams who are committed to truth and tenacity are not afraid to confront difficult issues, regardless of size. They win against sometimes unbelievably difficult odds and grow through their experiences. Their firm resolve to achieve is primarily noticed in their actions — the consistent proofs that principles in application count and can be counted upon.

Truth and tenacity do not exist apart from the firm dedication to the "Code of Achievement". Take away a sure and undeniable understanding of — and agreement with —

this code, and there is no consistent standard against which activity can be measured and success acclaimed.

Truth and tenacity are core characteristics of a work cluster where their code of achievement permeates the very fibers of their being and doing. A group who practices this code, because of who they are, is a Core Team.

The Story of James and Fulfilled Commitments

James is a personal friend with big dreams. We've worked together for a long time—first as part of a production team for a non-profit community service organization and then, on occasion, in consulting venues.

Many years of association and experience proved that when James made a promise, he fulfilled it. In fact, I don't think I've ever seen greater commitment shown to completion of an enterprise than when James was involved. He accomplished tasks faithfully and with excellence.

When we first became acquainted, he was a volunteer and I was a paid staff person. Our production team provided programming support for a series of live presentations, involving music, visuals, dance, dramatic arts, and technical support (sound and lights). We were privileged to work with many qualified personnel (professionals who volunteered their time and talents). Our team presented monthly shows often utilizing complex and integrated artistic elements. Our desires were to provide quality experiences for our audiences and effectively communicate the themes of the events. We achieved those goals repeatedly.

James was a volunteer, true, but I never saw more dedication from a man sold out to a cause, regardless of costs of time, energy, or money. He gave his full commitment time after time to assure success of our programming arts department. His contributions became the consistent "you can count on me" deliverable. Even when the demands of a production required our team to work into the very early morning hours, James was loyal and accountable. He demonstrated unfaltering allegiance to completion and closure.

As years went by, long after team members had moved on to other ventures, I would occasionally call on James and ask him to come tell his story, as part of our company's team-building seminars. Relating the history of our production team's commitment, cooperation, endurance and camaraderie, he would captivate and motivate our audiences as he relived the tales of thoughtful planning, hard work, quality achievements, and celebrated results.

But there was one aspect of his stories that could never be explained completely to people who weren't actually part of the occurrence. It was the extent to which our teams had adhered to truth and tenacity. Together we had often faced mounting challenges of too little equipment, insufficient time, awkward artistic personalities, conflicts with upper management, and not enough money.

In those tough times, James did not complain — rather, he complemented our team by making our jobs easier, regardless of circumstances. He personified confidence and care, communication and closure, reliability and accountability. The team on which he served shared and contributed from agreement on their values, vision, mission and message. This team built treasured and life-long friendships. Those relationships counted then and matter now.

It was true that if ever any of us wanted a job done well, there could be no better choice than to call on James. I found it to be so repeatedly, without variance.

Implementing truth and tenacity in the day-to-day dealings of a committed team is a worthwhile goal, but it is not necessarily achieved quickly. The journey of truthful living and tenacious working comes from, and is evidenced within the smaller but significant steps a core team takes to make their dreams of strength become secure positions of accomplishment. This process takes time.

A group's journey into this kind of significance combines and intertwines the journeys of the people who compose the team. Each person makes choices toward fulfillment of their group's mission on the basis of shared values and vision. Each individual learns valuable and life-embracing lessons that he or she imparts to others who want to listen and learn. These actions form living legacies, the verifiable proofs that core teams work because what they believe is shown in who they are, and what they contribute.

If a team like this could be manufactured, canned, created through the application of a magic formula, or put into a package to be sold to the highest bidder, the path of production might be convenient, but it wouldn't be right. Greatness can't be bought—it has to be won.

Greatness is seen in tough, long-lasting, right choices, those that bore through defeat and overcome difficult odds, building people while conquering. Victors in this business life investment model construct enduring relationships in which the supreme value of love is seen as a central and immovable trait. Love, the most meaningful relationship we can know, is the ultimate decision about another's success. It is readily observable in the dedication to help other persons achieve. Love is the cornerstone characteristic that a great core team strives to live out consistently.

A great core team's attitudes and actions, observed in their commitments to truth and tenacity, and to each other, are features that bring superior results for the persons who know that they are bound together in lasting endeavors. It is true: Love, evidenced in governing and growing relationships, never fails. Succeeding generations yearn to emulate the team who cares and builds one another in these ways.

Chapter 5:
Stovepipes, Silos, and the
Circle of Rights

The postmodern work habitat is a place of marked contrasts in atmospheres, attitudes, and actions. A close look reveals tensions between these opposites:

- Teams vs. individuals
- Cooperation vs. destructive competition
- Motivation vs. manipulation
- Deputizing vs. delegation
- Encouragement vs. intimidation
- Open communication vs. behind-the-back gossiping
- Truth vs. lies
- Solution provision vs. fault-finding
- Winning vs. whining
- Creativity vs. the status quo
- Innovation vs. rote performance
- Receptivity to change vs. resistance to change
- Forgiveness vs. holding grudges
- Profit vs. loss
- Fiscal freedom vs. debt
- Punctuality vs. lateness

- Faithfulness vs. slothfulness
- Diligence vs. laziness
- Commitment vs. disregard
- Choice vs. obligation
- Isolationism vs. cooperative engagement

This last one is the focus of this chapter.

Isolationism and Individualism

We will consider these two terms first. Their meanings are often confused.

For our purposes, "isolationism" is defined as the decision to be removed from cooperative relationships and functions. It is classified as an enemy of enhanced productivity when it prevents communication and cooperation. Isolationism inhibits strong individualism and teamwork.

"Individualism" describes a trait of self-confidence and assurance, born of good values. As the term is presented here, it does not include arrogance or self-absorption.

Individualism can exist within or apart from a team. Rugged individualism that features marked commitment and enduring strength originates from, and operates best within, a team environment where people are not islands unto themselves. Rugged individualists contribute most in a group where fresh thoughts and hard work are not inhibited or squelched, rather, welcomed and encouraged. A working cluster is not the enemy of robust individualism. A great core team is a place where strong individuals thrive and where expanded productivity is the result.

Isolationism and individualism are opposing forces. Each team member's vigorous individualism will contribute to the strength of everyone when a team labors together. When individuals cooperate, isolationism dies, and it should.

Two idioms often used to describe a lack of teamwork and open communication, are "stovepipe" and "silo." Both terms deserve attention by the core team that wants to condemn isolationism, encourage individual contributions, function in atmospheres of enriched communication, demonstrate cooperation, and fulfill responsibilities well.

The Stovepipe

I am acquainted with the owners of a hearth store in Iowa. They sell fireplaces and accessories, including stovepipes.

I had the privilege of interviewing the owner in preparation for *Core Teams Work Their Principles and Practices*. I wanted to talk about the stovepipes, and then extrapolate key points relating to business descriptions of the term.

You may have not thought about stovepipes lately, so here's the scoop. According to this businessman, "When a stovepipe is installed and utilized appropriately, it is useful and necessary.

"The stovepipe is crucially important in the overall safety and proper function of the heating system. In solid fuel combustion, many toxins are emitted. These toxins must be channeled to a safe location.

"The proper stovepipe is one made of materials that enable it to handle the environment to which it is being subjected. It must be the proper height to establish a natural draft. A good stovepipe will send harmful and potentially deadly toxins safely into the atmosphere.

"The particles channeled through the stovepipe accumulate over time, and this buildup must be addressed. At first glance, the stovepipe, from the outside, may look the same as it did the day it was installed. But it is critical that it is inspected carefully on the inside periodically. It is here that particle accumulation, if not dealt with on a regular basis, can create a catastrophic chain of events.

"After solid fuel combustion, some of the particulates (smoke) will begin to collect in the stovepipe. These particulates are still combustible and, under the right conditions, can cause a fire within the stovepipe itself, resulting in damage or possibly complete failure to the stovepipe, the system which it serves, and ultimately the entire dwelling in which it exists."

The stovepipe must be cleaned to maintain efficiency and ensure safety. The owner cautioned, "If care and maintenance are not given, not only will you no longer benefit from the heating system, but you will have to deal with the new set of problems left behind."

He continued, "To properly clean the stovepipe, assess what type of brush to use. There are several types — your choice depends on the kind or stage of build-up and the composition of the stovepipe.

"If the stovepipe is metal, a poly bristle brush is best suited. While a wire bristle brush will effectively clean the stovepipe, it will leave small scratches in the pipe, further reducing its lifespan. Under ideal burning conditions, a dry powdery build-up of creosote (the un-burned residue from solid fuel combustion) is deposited onto the inside walls of the stovepipe. This can be cleaned with a soft bristle brush of the appropriate size.

"If, however, the initial burning stage is not ideal, the effect is the presence of scaly, crystallized creosote. This substance must be removed using a wire brush. This wire brush will leave small scratch marks in the pipe, which will ultimately allow the creosote to build up more rapidly, resulting in higher maintenance.

"Finally, if the burning habits are poor, the creosote will liquefy. When it cools, it hardens and clings to the surface like an enamel finish. The process to remove this build-up is difficult and sometimes unsuccessful. In addition to aggressive brushing with a wire brush, a special acidic chemical is used to try to break down the composition of the glazed creosote.

"The life of the stovepipe has now been drastically compromised and the cost of maintenance has greatly exceeded the value of the stovepipe. In certain situations, it is more cost effective to simply replace it."

I asked, "What kind of attachment does a stovepipe installation require to assure that fumes do not get into a dwelling?"

The reply was this: "Properly fitted connections are all that are needed. Not all stovepipes are universal. Some brands are manufactured in a certain way, or to a certain size, which makes them unsafe to use with other brands. Know what you currently have and preferably stay with the same make rather than mix and match. Also, in the planning stages, the buyer should make sure to have access to additional parts should something break or wear out. It's much easier and economical to repair than it is to replace. Avoid getting something that is too unique or custom."

It is clear that the purpose of the stovepipe is to isolate and discard what we don't want, to keep the negatives away from the positives we desire to retain and enjoy. Further, to assure the quality and efficiency of operation, the device has to be kept clean.

Let's unpack the illustration. A stovepipe, when properly installed, utilized, and maintained, is a channel to rid an environment of unwanted particles brought about by combustion. It isolates the negative to create and enhance the positive. If we have stovepipes at all in the workplace they should be systems to isolate and rid ourselves of that which we don't want and never need, the adverse attitudes and actions that stifle or prevent successful team inner-workings.

Combustion happens when the heat is turned up, whether in physics, the office, or field. Conflicts occur within work environments. A great core team doesn't shy away from disagreements—it simply conducts them on appropriate levels, within frameworks of respect, dignity, courtesy, and commitment to each team member's success. When combustion occurs — and it will — a maturing core team knows what to get rid of and what to retain.

Cleaning is a part of maintaining and enhancing value for a stovepipe and a team. Every team faces issues where relationships and functions need to be refreshed if an organization is to succeed at building people and production. **Chapter 10 of *Core Teams Work*** lists twenty-one core issues for core teams. All of them are opportunities for improvement and all possess their own challenge points in a team's endeavor to achieve them. None of them can be dealt with in isolation. All of them require individual contributions of solution-minded people who cooperatively desire improvements in their workplaces, and who want to work together to achieve them.

A stovepipe that denotes and promotes isolationism in business is a wrong use of what otherwise could be a great symbol. A stovepipe that works as a channel for removal of waste is a far better application. Which does your team have?

Working Together

Curt Marshall led public sector strategic planning organizations for several U.S. Federal Government agencies for many years in Washington, D.C., and he is a good friend. Curt graciously agreed to be interviewed for *Core Teams Work.*

The focus of his interview was on the recurring problems that organizational "stove-piping" represents in the public and private sectors. His perspectives are revealing.

Five questions were posed.

1. *What is a stovepipe within public and private sectors?*

   "A stovepipe is an insular organization that does very little external gauging of what's going on outside its own somewhat closed environment. It pays very little attention to external stimuli. There is little interaction and communication between stovepiped organizations. They become fairly closed, often with little room for improvement, and sometimes even lose touch with their stakeholders."

2. *What are the negative results of stovepipes related to communication and deliverables processes?*

   "Communication across and within organizations does not flow freely. There often could be cross-cutting activities and strategic partnerships, positively affecting deliverables. But these are inhibited when stovepipes prevent interaction."

3. *What are the benefits when an organizational stovepipe is "cleaned" or removed?*

   "When a stovepipe is removed or the effect is reduced, we experience more interaction within the organization. Teams can form. A matrix-management-style organization can develop where people are inspired to work together in ways and areas that they may not have even thought of before."

4. *What kind of resistance should a leader or team participant expect when stovepipes are addressed?*

   "Resistance will exist because stovepipes are viewed as protection mechanisms. Status quo and power relationships are revealed. People who want to hide and maintain their protection mechanisms, can't. The security that existed in the status quo relationships will be challenged."

5. *When communication flows freely, what are the results?*

   "The results are often that entirely different deliverables are created that meet and/or exceed real world demands. The organization may produce greater than expected products from an expanded viewpoint when the stovepipe is reduced or eliminated. The organization has different conversations about what better outcomes can be achieved and deliverables are improved as a result. The organization becomes more transparent, and this leads to improved processes which often produce improved morale and better business results. This overall approach leads to a type of *learning organization* where all the participants benefit from the experience of working together, and where it is expected and acceptable for participants to challenge each other to improve their business processes."

The Silo

Jim Garlow is an author, conference speaker, media commentator, and a friend. He is also an authority on farming. Raised on a farm in Kansas, he has a wealth of knowledge and experience. In fact, in 1961 in his local community, he received the Future Farmers of America award for the tallest corn stock! Farming is simply a part of him—he has known its processes, buildings, and instruments well.

One agricultural building is the silo. Jim explained that basically there are two kinds. One is the cylindrical silo and the other, a trench silo. The cylindrical silo is indeed a cylinder, a tall one rising thirty, forty, up to fifty feet above the farm land. More modern ones are watertight and airtight. A trench silo is a ditch dug into the side of a hill, about the width of a truck.

The silo's primary purpose is to preserve crops for later use as feed. Silage, or ensilage, according to *The Colombia Electronic Encyclopedia*, is "…succulent, moist feed made by storing a green crop in a silo. The crop most used for silage is corn; others are sorghum, sunflowers, legumes, and grass. In a sealed silo … the crop ferments for about one month. This fermentation process, called ensiling, produces acids and consumes the oxygen in the silo, preserving the plant material. In pit ensiling, compacted silage ferments in an unsealed underground enclosure. Silage replaces or supplements hay for cattle, horses, and sheep. It is rich in carotene, an important source of vitamin A. A machine called an ensilage harvester cuts and chops the crop in one operation, preparing it for storage in the silo."

In business there is another kind of silo. In work environment applications, a silo refers to a habitat that prevents open communication. In commerce, silos are protective devices that are built to isolate people or departments from one another. Where these silos exist you can almost be assured that communication will be hindered, rumors will run rampant, gossip will be insidious, hidden agendas will pervade interaction, and people will refrain from offering assistance or engaging in open and productive communication, choosing instead to hinder and impede progress.

Silos used correctly, as they are on a farm, sustain life. Silos used incorrectly, as too often they are in business, suppress it.

Farm silos foster success because they represent effective and efficient handling of resources. Business silos hinder resourcefulness, prevent cross fertilization of creative ideas and solutions, and may destroy even the slightest potential for succeeding.

Jim and I agree: Let's keep the silos on the farm where they belong and will do the most good, for which they were designed in the first place. Remove them from your organization so people can communicate better and be enriched in the process.

You have a great and maturing team if none or few of its members are silo-makers. Great groups do not inhabit these kinds of closed, claustrophobic, stifling, and isolated environments. A great organization removes inhibitors of communication and creativity. Departments that work together make timely acquisition and application of appropriate information possible, probable, purposeful, recurring, and complete.

Tear down unhealthy business silos and replace them with across-the-board open communication, cooperation, and multiple-tiered achievement. Your team will grow, sustain life, and reproduce.

The Circle of Rights

Leaders and members of maturing teams want the right personnel to be engaged in the right activities within encouraging and cooperative work environments. It's a noble goal. To achieve it, the desire for right must be followed by intentional activity that positions the team's members for improved production.

In a millennium characterized by constant industrial advancements, more communication methods void of personal contact, and frequent technological re-inventions, maintaining and growing one-on-one interconnectivity is a challenge. Contemporary business activity breeds inhibitors to human interaction in its quest for a faster pace within far less space. But as was stated **on page 36 of** *Industrial Strength Solutions,* "Business may move at formerly unimaginable speeds of connectivity, but people still move at the pace of the heart, and it shall forever be so."

Within the challenge of treating people as people (instead of merely as implements for accelerated production) an opportunity exists for a core team to balance its relationships and functions. Leaders and followers share the responsibility to make great decisions about a team's success, to assure that right persons are well-placed to contribute great production, aligning deeds and needs. Correct positioning of people and production creates cooperation and needful construction. This harmonized state is another indicator of core team health.

Consider the **Circle of Rights on page 151.** The diagram illustrates balanced positioning. The quest is not to achieve or maintain a perfect equilibrium because, in fact, this perfection cannot be reached. There is always room for growth and flexibility. However, the prospect of moving toward this state is ever in front of the team who cares. It is a worthwhile objective toward which it perseveres.

Notice that there are six sections or right placements. All six should be present and carry equal weight for each team member. Where all six sections are close to being balanced with one another, a heightened degree of satisfaction exists within the individual.

The *right person* is one who is measuring up to the criteria listed **on pages 62 - 64 of *Leadership Is —*.** Right persons are people of impact and influence, who possess a track record of growing maturity and faithfulness, who are shown to be stable and accountable, who demonstrate humility and a teachable attitude, and whose life-season is appropriate to being able to receive and give leadership investment.

The *right place* is that station where the right person contributes out of health to produce wealth. In ***Industrial Strength Solutions***, beginning with **Chapter 6, page 149,** several tools are presented and explained to help the leader and the follower assure proper positioning and placement. **This chapter, entitled, "Strength Is a Condition — But It Is Not Conditional"** addresses positional perspectives, personnel placements, and performance procedures, including measurements of relational and functional behaviors.

The *right time* reminds us that identifying, allocating, and appropriately utilizing time, along with understanding correct operational timing, constitute responsible and required activities. Knowing the "when" is part of possessing good perspective and exercising wisdom in task fulfillment. As time and timing are carefully considered, doors open to reveal best judgments on how and when to accomplish needful movement. A right person in a right place looks for the right time to contribute his or her best.

Right motive originates from agreed and aligned core values. Motive is at the heart of the third question of The Four Questions restated in **"Getting Started" on page 21 of this book**. This third question asks, "What do you want?" The reason a team participant desires a position, action, placement, or opportunity says much about character and the value system that makes the contributor who he or she really is. The essence of the person is revealed in what he or she does.

Closely tied to the right place, the *right task* addresses competency. It includes desires for training, growth, expansion, and productivity. A team understands that right tasks are goal-achievement driven. Right task is all about function—making sure that a job is done well because the person doing it is best qualified.

Right reward refers to compensation. People who consider right reward know that payment is assured. Positioning payment to be commensurate with a job is an action never assumed; rather, it is deliberately and continually executed and evaluated. **On pages 56 and 57 of *Leadership Is—*, the "Law of Sowing and Reaping" and the "Law of Compensation" are discussed**. "The Law of Sowing and Reaping states that whatever leaders invest into the right soil will be multiplied back in a ratio of many to one. The Law of Compensation says that sure and compensatory reward will follow every action." The question that surrounds right reward is not whether payment is anticipated; instead, it asks what the payment should be for the effort expended. On a healthy core team the rewards will match not only the efforts of the contributor; they will also constitute heart-felt expressions of gratitude from those who value the people as people first and their contributions next.

The Circle of Rights is a standard toward which to strive and a measuring tool to evaluate success or failure, balance or imbalance. If you are a core team leader, introduce the Circle of Rights to your group to see how the team members measure up. Ask them to what degree they live and contribute within balance and how close their work experiences match the diagram.

Begin by drawing a circle without the internal dividing lines. Ask each team member to fill in their own pie chart reflecting what they believe their current status is as they view their presence and contributions. Then, upon review, develop steps to adjust toward balance, aligning with the Circle of Rights. Encourage each team member to become a true reflection of your team's desires for best people and placements, so that everyone in the group — because they are more important than what they do — is best positioned for success, relationally and functionally.

A team unafraid to confront imbalance with truth will engage in activities to correct a lack of symmetry. In fact, an exercise of this kind will demonstrate desires for positive contribution, and will create health as the process unfolds. Open communication, truthful evaluation, and timely responses encourage favorable results. These are the principles employed when imbalance is adjusted toward balance.

Because the process is more important than the product, consistently weigh your workplace paradigms against the example of the Circle of Rights. It's in the process of evaluation and adjustment that maturity develops. Growth, from renewed perspectives and needful modifications, should be an ongoing by-product.

The Circle of Rights

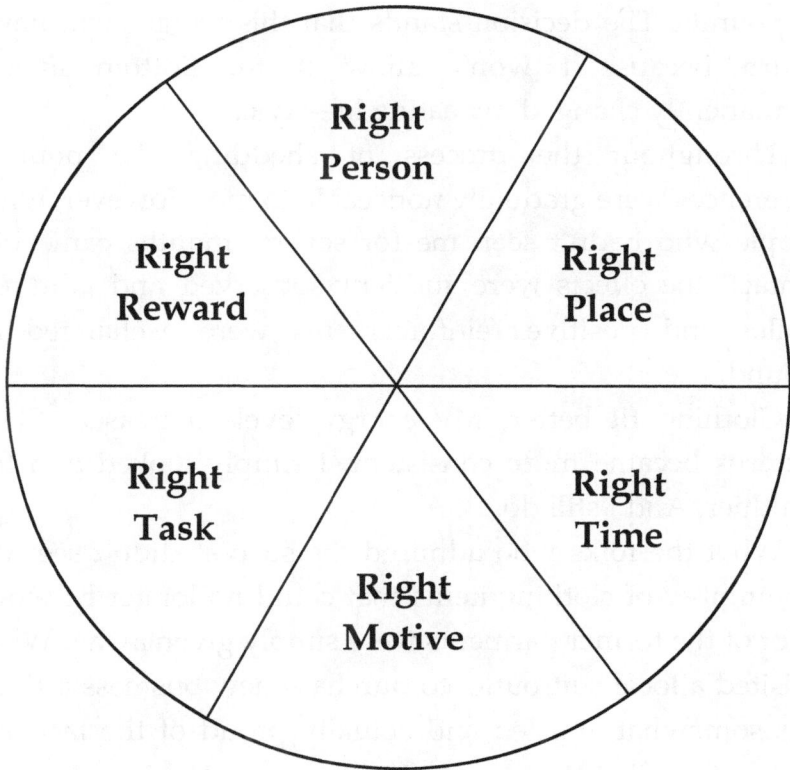

Right
Person

Right
Place

Right
Reward

Right
Time

Right
Task

Right
Motive

---

*Question for your team: How willing would you and your team
be to engage in forthright and respectful discussions about
applying the Circle of Rights as a standard to which to aspire
and a grid of measurement along the way?*

In early 2011 I made a life-style choice to lose and refuse unwanted and potentially detrimental weight, encouraged by family. Over the course of four years, through diet adjustments and applying common sense, I was able to drop 67 pounds. The decision stands that this weight will never return because I won't allow it to. Bottom line: I permanently changed my eating life-style.

Throughout the process of shedding the pounds, differences were gradually noticeable to me. However, when people who hadn't seen me for several months came into contact, the effects were suddenly observed and admired. Smiles and positive reinforcements were exchanged all around.

Clothing fit better. My energy levels increased. Sleep patterns became more consistent. I simply looked and felt healthier. And I still do.

What the folks who admired the success didn't see was the number of clothing items that could no longer be worn. A lot of the former garments were simply given away. When I visited a local suit outlet to purchase new business attire, I was somewhat amazed and actually proud of the fact that the sizes needed then were nowhere near the sizes that had been.

The point, you ask? A proper fit is important. Whether for a coat or in consideration of a position on a team, the fit should be, well, right.

When You Fit

When you fit, your world becomes far more balanced and manageable. When you fit, you are not isolated. You are included. Your contributions are wholesome and desired.

When you fit, you look and act better. The health and worth of your offerings are noticeable and verifiable. You receive affirmation and the honor that comes from achieving balance personally and with the team on which you serve.

When you fit, you are motivated to learn more, earn more, and give more away. You become a maturing student and example maker, providing nurture, support, encouragement, and excellence. Your accountability increases, as does the confidence other people on your team express in you. Your faithfulness is not questioned. Your word is verified.

When you fit, you become more authentic — the same person to everyone, no masks, charades, hidden agendas, or behind-the-scenes maneuvering. When you fit, you become part of a growing group of people who make mutual decisions about one another's successes and communicate them well.

When you fit, you know it.

When You Don't Fit

When you don't fit, your garments — what people see that are parts of your outward image (attitudes, expressions, moods) — do not feel good, nor do they promote your best.

Working with you becomes the sour hour for team members. They tread lightly, afraid to rattle you.

When you don't fit, you may engage in gratuitous behavior, more of a required exercise like paying an imposed tax, instead of freely giving offerings of solid work ethics out of appreciation and affirmation. When you don't fit, the ground rules may be more about getting by, barely meeting expectations functionally (your actions), whether or not you agree relationally (in terms of your decisions) with the values and principles of the group. What you do is more by force than a matter of willful and purposeful course.

When you don't fit, you may dwell in isolated atmospheres of frustration and failure instead of environments of fortitude and faith. Discouragement may take up unlawful and needless residence.

When you don't fit, you will probably struggle with change — especially to your position or portion. Complaining can take the place of commitment, whining the place of winning.

When you don't fit, you may stretch or bend the rules for selfish acquisition, adopting an "I don't care" attitude. Negativity and defeatism may become parts of your daily contributions to the workings of the team.

When you don't fit you should want to create something better for yourself and your associates. You will, if you earnestly desire to be a part of an organization that contributes from health. If you desire positive and contributory change, you will yearn for balance and strive with your team to acquire and live within it.

How important is a proper fit? It is vital to life and prosperity — for you and those with whom you serve.

Your team will mature and contribute more effectively if they refuse stovepipes and silos, replacing them with people-groups who contribute out of proper placements as shown in the Circle of Rights, where group members strive to fit well and contribute out of strong and enduring relationships. Remember, isolationism and cooperative engagement are not partners.

Chapter 6:
Team Communication —
Examples that Endure

Effective communication is an extremely important principle and practice — perhaps the most essential characteristic and evidence of core team health. It is *the* pathway for the team that wants to build great people and improved production. See if the following interview resonates with you.

Judy and Communication in the Media

Judy is a media communications professional and has been a friend for several years. The organizations she has led have been CTRG clients, and she is a trainer of CTRG principles. She has overseen and managed many media sales teams, and has served as a general manager for two radio stations in a major United States market.

In her interview for *Core Teams Work Their Principles and Practices*, Judy and I honed in on the topic of communication, what many believe is the most basic need of any team. I asked her several questions about her leadership of core teams and the role that great communication plays in achieving desired results.

1. *Which core team principles are most important to you for the effective operation of a team?*

   "The principles that I value most are these: People are more important and valuable than the jobs they do, the process is more important than the goal, closing loops is essential, leaving a meeting with clear direction for everyone involved is important."

2. *As a leader, what do you expect from consistent application of these core team principles?*

   "I expect a positive domino effect throughout the team, starting with the person at the top, and a change in attitude and action towards other team members based on effective communication."

3. *What are some of the obstacles that a leader faces in trying to teach and apply core team principles, and how are they overcome?*

   "One obstacle is breaking old habits. Most employees have been managed by fear and conclude that they must hide their feelings and input, believing that they will be ridiculed or seen as complainers if they do speak up. Lack of communication is the biggest obstacle a manager faces, not just with him or herself and the employees, but between employees as well. Once an employee feels safe enough to communicate openly and honestly with other employees about frustrations, and offer solutions, a huge hurdle has been overcome. This line of direct communication must be implemented on a consistent basis by the manager in order for it to become common practice with his or her employees."

4. *When a core team works well, an entire organization is affected. What is an example of this in your experience?*

"When I resigned my position as general manager of two national network radio stations, the greatest reward was hearing my staff say to me, 'You taught me so much about communicating, being a good listener, treating others with respect, and asking people for their best efforts. I always wanted to work hard for you and make you proud, and myself proud, too.' This was the best reward and gift I could have asked for."

Open and honest communication in an encouraging environment is the central idea. Judy's leadership reflects her dedication for her followers to succeed, by promoting this best practice. Leaders who want more communication must model what they want in order to enjoy the results they desire.

Increased and improved communication is a common need for organizations that desire improvement. Of the twenty-one challenge areas we have identified as core issues most core teams face **(see pages 227 – 245 of *Core Teams Work*),** this one resides close to the top spot every time.

What makes up good or great communication? How does a core team know that communication is working well, especially when identifying failures to communicate is so common?

You are invited to review the explanation of **open lines of communication** as described in *Leadership Is—* **pages 100 - 108. On pages 106 and 107**, this vital tool is a required practice for problem solving. It is seen as a factor in creating realistic expectations of results **on page 111**. Effective communication is part of the **"Twelve Laws of Understanding," found on pages 145 - 155**. It is essential to a mentoring process, **described on pages 176 - 183. Listening,** a necessary action within communication is **highlighted on page 189. And on page 224, communication and closure** are positioned as interactive elements within operational systems, the considerations of any leader who wants to finish well.

In *Industrial Strength Solutions*, **communication** is referenced as a part of faithful completion of tasks on page **96**, as a first priority item of **solution provision on page 111**, and as the goal of effective **blending of core team success factors on page 125**. Positive and contribution-focused relational behaviors include **active communication, as related on pages 184 and 188**. It is listed as a **proof of effective function on pages 190 and 191**. Communication is positioned as a value and a valued practice for a team who wishes to remain strong when adversity strikes, as noted in the story, **"The Walled City," on pages 199 - 206**. When the four attributes of industrial strength solutions are chosen—namely holistic view, wholeness, humility, and firm resolve—critical communication channels are opened and produce fusion of relationship and function, as noted on **pages 207 – 223**.

So let's define the term "communication." Communication is sharing information that promotes behavioral change, the results of which become known to appropriate parties. Communication is not fully completed unless behaviors change, hopefully for the better.

Communication is an art, much like other values whose practice may not be a science, but whose results are evidentiary. Proofs of great communication can be seen in multiple applications. Several are considered here, including conversations, meetings, the process of fulfillment, confidentiality and obtaining permission, and the growth of your people.

The Elements of a Good Conversation

I have extensive experience, as a professional musician, in orchestration and performance. Creating and presenting intriguing musical arrangements for voices and instrumentation are parts of a goal of crafting musical "conversations" that are inviting and meaningful.

Musical art is best achieved when one element plays off of, or responds to, another. A flowing and harmonically sensitive score will utilize moving parts of one instrument, or section, to ask questions to which other instruments or sections will provide answers. Or, one vocal or instrumental group will make musical statements that elicit interjections from alternating singers or players. Vocal arrangements, most often, are tied to the lyrics of a piece, and an effective orchestral arrangement, combining vocal and instrumental parts, should mirror the message the composer wants to communicate to the listener. Composition and arranging of this kind draws the player and the listener into the intent of a song and makes for superb communication when accomplished well.

Communication is the goal of any conversation, musical or otherwise. In this state of interaction the parties are educated, inspired, informed, included, and called to respond.

Positive and healthy conversations represent great opportunities for interchange and interaction when certain fundamental traits are present. Among them are the following:

1. Affirmation originating from mutual respect
2. Awareness of the needs of the speaker and listener
3. Adopting an open mind and receptive demeanor
4. Active listening where genuine attention is paid to the participants
5. Asking relevant questions that demonstrate focus and interest
6. Answering questions openly and honestly
7. Accenting the ebb and flow of the exchange, realizing that healthy conversations are dynamic, not static
8. Appreciating the people who are engaged (usually by telling them)
9. Allowing ample space for completion of thoughts and expressions
10. Attentive interest when diverse opinions are considered

11. Abiding in the focus points and minimizing distractions
12. Agreeing when possible, and politely offering and expressing differing views when you can't

Equally important in a good conversation is a list of negative behaviors to avoid. Several are listed here:

1. Disrespect
2. Interruptions — especially those that originate from rudeness
3. Needless argumentation
4. Out-of-control tempers
5. Dwelling on topics that have already been closed
6. Allowing or restating out-of-date, negative, unfortunate, and possibly forgotten agendas, to prove a point
7. Distractions that show non-interest or disconnect
8. Dissention and disruptive attitudes
9. Unnecessary repetition
10. Monopolizing or talking over another person
11. Failing to listen
12. Closed or closeted minds
13. Selfishness
14. Whining
15. Fault-finding and blaming
16. Negativity
17. Refusal to hear alternative views
18. Inattentiveness
19. Ignorance
20. Lack of preparation

21. Attitudes of superiority or one-upmanship
22. Allegations and accusations presented without proper research and sufficient opportunity for thoughtful responses
23. Defensiveness
24. Manipulation
25. Placation
26. Gossip
27. Sarcastic put-downs
28. Lies and misrepresentations
29. Intimidation
30. Verbal abuse
31. Ostracism
32. Attacks
33. Lack of courtesy
34. Denial of dignity
35. Dishonor

Notice that mutual respect begins the list of positive conversation traits and that disrespect is at the forefront of negative behaviors. The presence or absence of respect is at the center of healthy or unhealthy interchange. Uplifting or degrading results flow from these corresponding conditions.

The potential for a good and productive conversation exists when the parties involved commit to exercising mutual respect as a condition of engagement. Clearly, the opposite is also true: Where commitment to mutual respect is not present, positive conversation will most likely fail. When respectful conversation stops, uplifting communication ceases.

It may seem obvious, but articulating the rules of the game, including the positive attributes above, provides a framework into which parties can contribute their thoughts and ideas, if the participants agree on the rules, and decide to obey them. If your team struggles with how they converse, review the lists of desired and undesired behaviors. The team may see where they excel, and note what changes they must make, to more effectively engage in beneficial conversation.

Meetings

A group setting provides another opportunity to engage in productive information sharing. Core team meetings are occasions when great communication can take place.

At CTRG we teach a 50/50 formula for implementing a productive meeting. Up to 50% of the meeting's content and focus should be relational, and up to 50% of the meeting should be functional.

Remember that a relationship is defined as the decision one makes about another's success. The relationally-driven part of a core team meeting examines, corrects, and celebrates the decisions that the members have made about each other and their networks. These networks often include other teams, vendors, and customers. Within these relationship-based discussions the team looks at its values, value system, vision, and message to assure that their actions openly portray what this team really wants. Conversation revolves around how better decisions can be made to help others on the team succeed, in what formats and time frames these decisions will be implemented, and who will own them. A maturing core team eagerly anticipates and looks forward to these interactions.

Function is the other essential ingredient on a productive core team's agenda. Function is all about the mission of the group, the tasks it has accomplished, the needful responsibilities that are yet to be completed, and the methods the group will employ to bring fulfillment and closure. Function is the child of strong and growing relationships, so it is easy to see that, when function emerges from values-driven ties, the motivation to innovate and achieve excellence is a natural outcome.

Teams that are function-driven may accomplish much. They will accomplish more, however, and grow their people through the process, when the tasks they do are true reflections of solid relational decisions. These quality decisions produce frameworks in which functions required for success are exercised.

Here are ten relationship-driven functions that help a meeting succeed:

1. The person who calls the meeting is generally the one responsible for the creation of its contents.
2. Each meeting has an agenda, published to the participants in advance.
3. Only people who need to be at a meeting are requested to be there. We don't waste anyone's time.
4. Participants are on time and ready to engage from the outset with note-taking implements or tablets.

5. Preparation is required from each team member to assure that time is used efficiently when the group comes together.

6. Minutes of a preceding meeting are read and action steps evaluated.

7. Reports are succinct.

8. Needs for further deliberation on any item may require additional meetings for selected members, so the meetings are scheduled, and personal responsibilities are assigned. (See *Industrial Strength Solutions*, **pages 162 and 163.**)

9. Action plans are recorded and include responsible parties for task fulfillment, a timeline of accomplishment, the reporting structure for communication loop closure (see below), and an evaluation method.

10. A designated team member creates a summary of the meeting's content and action plans, communicating this to the participants and others who need to know (usually via email or other written method), to assure understanding and assignment of responsibilities.

Every group session needs a concise conclusion. How do you close your group's meetings? At CTRG we offer this procedure to W.R.A.P. up a meeting:

1. W- Wind it up on time. Show respect for other people and their schedules.

2. R- Review the context and content, thanking members for their participation and contributions.

3. A- Apprise the team of agreed and assigned responsibilities, along with associated timelines.
4. P- Plan for the next meeting. Assure that the participants know when and where it is to be conducted, what its purpose, procedures, and expected outcomes will be.

Communication Loop Closure: The Process of Fulfillment

We covered closure in **Chapter 4** and, in a process of good communication, closure is a key element. For example, let's say that core team member A requests or requires an action step from core team member B, a common occurrence. What are the responsibilities that B has in the fulfillment of the task?

Concluding that B is accountable, then the task will be fulfilled. But is the process fully completed when the work is done? Depending on the nature of the task and its degree of importance, it may not be.

The rule of thumb is this: The task is not completed until the assigning party (in this case A) knows that it has been completed because A has been informed by B that this is so. If A has to chase B for information as to completion of a task, then two factors emerge:

1. A has not trained B on the required process of reporting, if the expectation is that the communication loop should be closed.
2. If B has been informed of the expectation of reporting, then B is not following well, is clearly not owning

responsibility, and is de-valuing the relationship with A, making a decision not in support of A's success.

Of course, there are variations on this theme which you will apply to your situation. The central focus point is that responsible action will include communication that assures knowledge of completion.

In the **diagram on page 170,** several action steps are presented involving persons A and B. Here are their responsibilities:

1. Participate in a neutral (non-emotional) assimilation of facts, assuring understanding of what is requested or required.
2. Establish and state the reasons for the directive and declare what actions will ensue.
3. Consider the message that is conveyed and the methods and communication styles being chosen, to assure accuracy.
4. Agree and decide on appropriate action.
5. Create and declare a timeline for fulfillment.
6. Perform the requested action and fulfill the roles and responsibilities with excellence.
7. Decide when and how the team or assigning party will *know* that the action is fully completed.
8. Close the loop. Closure occurs when the member assigned informs the assigning person that the action has been completed.
9. Evaluate, to ascertain what improvements may be required.

10. Appreciate and celebrate. Affirmation follows a job finished with excellence.

Responsible action will include communication that assures knowledge of completion.

Team member A assigns a task to B.
What are the responsibilities?

Fulfillment of Assigned Tasks

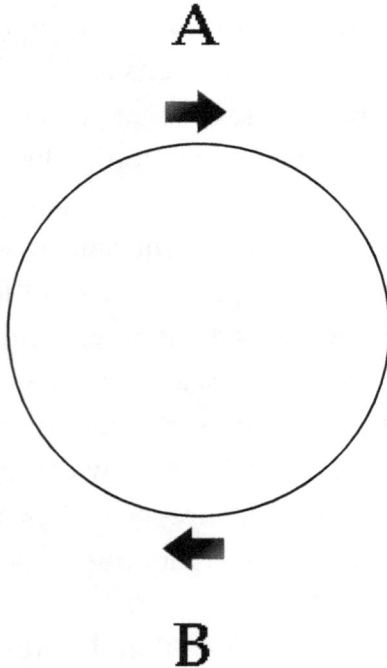

A

B

The Process of Fulfilment of Assigned Tasks

1. Participate in a neutral (non-emotional) assimilation of facts, assuring understanding of what is requested or required.
2. Establish and state the reasons for directives, and declare what actions will ensue.
3. Consider the message that is conveyed and the methods and communication styles being chosen, to assure accuracy.
4. Agree and choose an appropriate action.
5. Create and declare a timeline for fulfillment.
6. Perform the requested action and fulfill the roles and responsibilities with excellence.
7. Decide when and how the team or assigning party will know that the action is fully completed.
8. Close the loop. Closure occurs when the member assigned informs the assigning person that the action has been done.
9. Evaluate, to ascertain what improvements may be required.
10. Appreciate and celebrate. Affirmation follows a job finished with excellence.

Confidentiality and Obtaining Permission

Confidentiality is paramount in many business engagements. Sensitive information may require it and, when it is mandated, the people of the healthy and maturing core team honor it unequivocally. There may be multiple reasons for confidentiality that, on the surface, may not be fully understood; regardless, trust is respected and firmly upheld as part of good communication.

Let's define "confidentiality." Confidentiality is holding to yourself the information entrusted to you.

Keeping a secret in positive circumstances can be just as challenging as keeping your mouth shut in more difficult ones. But troubling, thorny, or upsetting circumstances, not in violation of law, may require the leader to get to the bottom of a matter if positive resolution is desired. The need for confidentiality must be balanced with requirements to uncover or disclose pertinent information. This can be difficult to do. Negative incidents (undesirable events), if not dealt with appropriately, can give rise to growing discomfiture and dysfunction, so they must be handled. The key is to handle them well.

Teams who respect confidentiality and exercise mutual respect desire to uncover incidents and discover issues behind the events, and do this in best ways. One preferred method is to request permission for disclosure and discussion. In positive resolution environments delving deeper occurs after permission has been requested and obtained from the parties involved, demonstrating attitudes of respect, openness, and truth-telling. More often than not, asking for and granting permission represents a superior mode of uncovering and dealing with unsettling information.

Clearly, there are situations when requesting another's permission is not the right choice. When relationships have been severed, or function is proved to be unethical, not in line with values and standards, or decidedly wrong, then a leader may have to invade without permission.

When it's possible, however — and most of the time it is — request. Respect the people in your quest to ascertain the facts you need to repair incidents, resolve issues, and restore relationships. Remember, when quality decisions are ongoing parts of team activity, utilizing permission is natural, honors knowledge, validates perspectives, showcases trust, and treats people with dignity.

Inquiring, "May I have your permission to talk about this with you, your co-worker, or supervisor?" can open the door to refusal as well as agreement, of course. But if you are the one asking for the opportunity to acquire the facts to help create solutions on behalf of the people involved, you will declare through your respectful actions that you can be trusted. Honoring confidentiality grows confidence.

Growth of Your People — The Lessons of an Executive

Mary Walker was General Counsel of a large U.S. Federal Government legal staff and a superb leader. She graciously consented to be interviewed for this book.*

> *Mary Walker's viewpoints reflect a government context and therefore may not include private sector options.

She exercised superior communication with her staff to help train, encourage, inspire, and congratulate them. Communication performed in this way, with a tandem view of growing people and their contributions, is clearly a solid model.

The major focus of our interview was this: How do you motivate your staff, and what are the expectations of results from these efforts?

I asked her four questions:

1. *What are the hallmarks of a great team that you have led?*

   Mary spoke of shared vision, seeing the big picture of what is needed, what is possible, desired, and what the team can accomplish together, whether meeting a customer or an organizational need. "The vision for what is possible originates from the leader, but can reflect ideas of team members who also sense the need for change and adjustment."

   Shared loyalty is another hallmark. Loyalty shown to each other on the team is evidenced in affirming conversation, declaration of commitment, recognition and positive engagement in hard work, and celebration of results. Loyalty promotes keeping the end-view in mind, as well as providing a common defense against those who would criticize or minimize attempts at change.

Another sign of a great team "…is the energy demonstrated in the ideas and initiatives department: once team members capture the vision they will produce and create ideas toward achieving the vision."

Question for your group: How much do they share vision, demonstrate loyalty, and engage in creative solution provision?

---

2. *When a team is at high operational efficiency, how does the leader know?*

   "The first sign is receiving customer feedback and responding to it. The results show that our people are performing well and at optimal levels, that customer needs are being met in new ways that are desired. Next, that staff and clientele are happy with organizational and positive changes, seen in client comments." Mary noted that some clients do not like change and will resist it, so it is important to have them in the minority. How true. "Process flows are more efficient and smoother, attitudes are positive, full talents are engaged and a lot of high quality work is getting done. Indeed, output with excellence is enhanced.

   "Developments of legacies are proactive and solution-oriented, dedicated to building people to take our places through multiple layering and mentoring. This kind of building promotes quality now and in the future.

"In our organization mentoring is seen in creation of 5-year training programs for each staff member, associated educational processes, and developmental assignments." An example of the positive effects of mentoring in Mary's group is a summer clerk program that is so successful that many more candidates are applying than can be accepted and the program is viewed as very attractive.

Finally for this question, modeling. Mary models what she wants by taking people appropriately into her trust. Integrity is evidenced in upfront confidence that is built on truth and good judgment.

Questions for your team: What are the signs of your operational efficiency? How much customer feedback do you seek? How smooth-running are your operations and to what degree of excellence is the work being fulfilled? What kinds of legacies is your team building? How much mentoring occurs? How duplicative is leadership modeling on your team?

---

3. *How much, if at all, should a leader have to track down employee contributions and task fulfillment?*

The answer, ideally, was "none." A leader should never *have* to track information down. Mary's desire of her staff is that they keep her informed of what she needs to know to do her job and make the entire office look good.

The leader wants the followers to own responsibility by anticipating the leader's needs, and Mary tries to model this. "Impediments are responses characterized by failing to report or deliver on time, usually stemming from stubbornness or laziness, and a 'lone-wolf' syndrome that says, 'I can do it on my own; I don't need you...' which is mainly a demonstration of arrogance more than anything. "Rewards are commensurate with the degree of ownership a follower has, of not needing to be tracked down, and of delivering appropriate and timely messages and advice. The person who does these becomes a trusted advisor.

"We divide responsibilities to build synergy — accomplishing something that working together will fulfill far better than working in silos." Mary talked about requiring various divisions to work together to produce something they could not do alone, and appointing the one most likely to accomplish the task as the "head" of the effort.

"When given a cooperative assignment, each division has some responsibility for work that affects all of the divisions, and will be judged by how well they accomplish that. The idea is to get them to think on behalf of the entire organization, not just their component part."

Questions for your team: How much, if any, does your team's leadership have to track down employee contributions and task fulfillment? To what degree do team members anticipate each other's needs? How does your team handle stubbornness and laziness or a team participant who engages in isolationism? Who are your team's trusted advisors? What are the projects that your team uses to build synergy through cooperation? What opportunities are you able to provide to your people who want to grow and expand their horizons?

---

4. *What methods have you employed and seen bear fruit to encourage employees to become committed to task completion and communication loop closure?*

   Mary listed several means that have worked for her and her staff. One was assigning due dates and requiring that staff hold themselves accountable to them. Another was giving rewards commensurate with performance as a part of positive reinforcement.

   Mary meets twice a year with each of her top leaders and followers to speak truth in an atmosphere of relational caring, but dialogs more frequently on individual assignments as to what is needed and expected.

   She also praises great contributions openly, in the presence of peers and others. And she assigns more responsibility to those who have proven they can produce, where this greater responsibility will grant them the opportunity for more prestige and respect.

> *Questions for your team: Which of the above methods do you employ with the people on your team? How important is openly showing praise of accomplishment in front of peers and other persons of significance?*

Effective communication adheres to core team principles. It produces positive and recurring benefits when practiced consistently. Negative habits are broken and affirmations flow as people grow through the process.

Remember the definition: Communication is sharing information that promotes behavioral change, the results of which become known to appropriate parties. Communication is not fully completed unless behaviors change, hopefully for the better.

Great examples of beneficial communication are good conversations, effective meetings, and the process of fulfillment of assigned tasks. In resolving difficult issues, respecting confidentiality and requesting permission are staples of a healthy communication environment.

Your team can know it is communicating well when people mature, contribute within strengthened relationships, and provide excellent production. Doing communication right has great and enduring rewards.

Chapter 7:
Rehearsal and Performance —
A Customer Service Model

Core Teams Work Their Principles and Practices presents a business life investment model. Within this model, the staff comes first. Customer needs are met best when provision comes from a well-served staff. The opposite is not true. Great customer service does not automatically originate from staff personnel who are used up. Plainly stated, the customer is not, and should not be, first in priority. What the customer receives will be excellent in attitude and quality if and when the staff serving the customer is treated in these ways initially by the staff's leadership. Invest at home first. Provide service to customers through your people, not in spite of them.

This model generates positive and duplicative behaviors. This model transfers ownership of quality customer service *into* a staff because the staff has first seen the validity of service-heart action *from* the leadership and wants to share what it has received *with* the people it serves.

Leadership invests what it wants returned and holds itself accountable *to* the staff before ever requiring accountability *from* them. This model benefits all it touches.

These transferable actions don't just happen. They must be rehearsed so that they can be performed well, not unlike the musician who practices diligently so that the presentation can be as close to flawless as possible when the recital comes.

Creating duplicative models is necessary in building teams that function for the right reasons and last beyond the immediate. When people act upon principle they know their actions must fully align with the guidelines upon which their core teams are built and to which they are dedicated. Their model is transferred when they inspire others to repeat what they have done.

There are no effective substitutions for the principled investments that a leader of a great core team gives to his or her staff. Relational authenticity is revealed from the very first day when a core team member sees a leader work to embody life truths in consistent application, especially in customer service activity — where the staff is the leader's customer.

The order is important. Leaders give to staff. Staff gives to those they serve. Customers are served best when the staff is served first.

Setting these priorities of investment is required of leadership and, frankly, it is hard work, but worth it. If you are the leader, recognize these fundamental truths, rehearse them, and then perform them.

1. People willingly follow because they see a leader cares more about them than just their programs or productivity.

2. Core teams who are healthy are composed of leaders and followers who understand the priority of investing in staff before fulfilling customer needs, providing models of how people should be treated regardless of whether they are buying or selling.
3. Pouring efforts into staff for development and actualization of values in day-to-day experience shows the staff how to serve the customer.
4. Leaders who use up their staff to meet customer demands are not validating the truth of "People are more important than what they do." In the process of violating this truth they undercut the very strengths that otherwise would create more expanded health.

Customers are served best when the staff is served first.

Customer Service Initiatives (CSI)

CSI is a way of thinking and acting. It focuses on the provider before seeking to meet the needs of the provisioned. Seen from the perspective of measuring results, the degrees of success of the former become the guarantee of fulfillment of the latter.

A sequential order is important and is unalterable. Customers are going to be served, regardless. Within the core team model, the focus point is not the end result; rather, it's the process of arriving there. Because the process is more important than the product, and the people more important than production, it stands to reason that investment in providers as the first priority causes two results: maturing people and greater provision, in that order.

Teaching a staff, a core team of service providers, that they are more important than what they do, becomes a lesson these same people teach their customers: that the customers are more important than what they buy. People who embrace and act upon this truth develop character traits like trust, loyalty, unity, confidence, and accountability. These traits cause service providers to try to excel to even higher degrees of customer satisfaction, and the customers know it—and return for more. It's a cycle that benefits all.

Quality customer provision requires that the people serving the customer take the initiative to do it right. Seven CTRG Customer Service Initiatives are listed below. If these truths resonate with you and your team, you are invited and encouraged to use them.

1. *Teach* the core team that the ways they want to be treated are the ways they will treat each other and their customers. This is the Golden Rule, of course. It works.

2. *Implant* the values and principles of the core team into every transaction—those between team members and with customers.

3. *Apply* your team's value system, like the "Twelve Laws of Understanding" **(see page 207)** to personal and personnel dealings.

4. *Declare* your values—the principles on which your team agrees—to team members and customers. The

lists for the team and the customers it serves should be identical, even though their expressions (the languages that are chosen to best communicate to the targets) may vary.

5. *Communicate with your target.* Because you desire to know them well, use languages they speak, to assure understanding.

6. *Dedicate yourself* to providing a model of follow-through, closure-inclusive communication, and fulfillment. This dedication proves accountability and stability.

7. *Openly demonstrate* superior customer service provision within your team initially, and return these best practices to the customer.

Profit is a measurable marker of success. While it is true that profit may be viewed only as pecuniary gain, within CSI, relationships' profit is seen on more than one level. It is present first on behalf of the people who are engaged in the process of delivery—their growth, maturity, confidence, competence, and the exercise of the values they have agreed to embrace. Secondly, profit is seen as a result of this investment in the customer, who not only receives a product or service, but is better for the experience, as is the provider who receives a pecuniary reward.

CSI works when a team's actions are based on enduring values. Investment in a core team's success originates from the leader when he or she cares more about the team than comfort, image, position, title, or tenure. Care is apparent when it is demonstrated in every stage of development of core team structure and operation. What binds the core team together applies to the relationships of a staff and its customer base. What is learned and modeled on the team is taught and modeled with the customer.

It is never too late to begin a customer servicing operation like this. It's a journey of development, a quest that is worth the energy, especially when the team's customer service provision quotients rise to levels the leader may have never even thought possible.

If you are the leader, or a follower who wants to become one, then look to a leader who is doing it well for an example of how to do it right. The story of Rob Sweet's police officer training may serve to encourage you as you grow your people, investing in them because they are more important than what they do.

Rob Sweet, Training Officer for Police Recruits

Rob Sweet is a training officer for one of the major law enforcement police academies in the United States. During his career he has trained over eighteen thousand recruits. He is a dedicated leader, team player, and personal friend. I count it a privilege to have interviewed him for *Core Teams Work Their Principles and Practices.*

The tasks inherent in police work require dedication to building effective work groups. Rob's training highlights some of the essential characteristics of constructing and operating a solid core team.

Here is his interview:

1. *Recognizing that you have been responsible for training over eighteen thousand police officers in a time frame covering eight years, what is your primary motivation when a new class starts?*

   "My primary goal on day one is to set a high standard of professionalism in front of every member of the team. This is done by exercising command presence in appearance, attitude, and demeanor. I will look like a leader and act like it. I set the standard."

2. *How important is team loyalty to your recruits when they first start a class with you and later when you are finished training them?*

   "From the first minute that the recruits are at the academy I set them up as a team and begin exercises to begin building teamwork. They learn immediately how to depend on each other. Without teamwork the class could not function efficiently.

   "The staff sets the example of teamwork and we continually put the recruits in situations where they learn that teamwork equates to 'economy of movement.' They learn that empowerment, assigning tasks, and responsibility, are important elements to teamwork. They learn that team loyalty is vital in police work, that, in fact, lives depend on it.

   "When the final weeks of class roll around, team loyalty is integrated into daily practices. Recruits help each other without anyone asking them to do so. This is gratifying to me and the staff. Our examples and teachings have paid off. This is a big accomplishment for the recruits and, at that point, they are ready for the next phase of training."

3. *What parts do positive correction and reinforcement of good behavior play in your training operations?*

"There are different stages of positive correction and reinforcement of good behavior within the eighteen weeks of basic training. The academy is a semi-militaristic environment. There is a good deal of pressure that is initially placed on recruits to check personality and illustrate the outcome of poor performance. If there are numerous errors in performance there is personal 'attention.' When performance improves, then the amount of personal attention is reduced, causing a positive reinforcement of good behavior.

"Positive reinforcement of good behavior is coupled with 'good effort' and 'good work' reinforcements. As the weeks progress, the sharp structured environment is somewhat smoothed.

"When recruits do not perform a function of their job correctly we illustrate the possible outcomes that could occur were this done on the streets, and how it could place someone's life in danger or tarnish the public trust in police work. We show the recruits the correct way and they perform the scenario until they accomplish the task correctly, with reinforcing words from the team and the staff."

4. *How do you view your trainees from the first day and all the way through the process?*

"When I first see the class on Monday morning, I see a group of diverse people who are coming together for one purpose—to give back to the community in which they live and to perform tasks which no one else can or would perform to make their communities safer.

"The desires that brought each of them here have taken great courage to fulfill. They are not doing this for money or fame. I see a group of people who are eager to learn how to do police work. They have overcome numerous obstacles to get to this point. They are determined to do what it takes to succeed, yet they must be submissive enough to accept the challenges.

"As the weeks progress we see changes in paradigm and character. We are not looking for robots but individuals who have compassion and drive—people who are able to work with limited supervision in total confidence. Toward the end of basic training, we see people who are much more alert, cautious, but a little more aggressive.

"Let me give you my personal example of how I used to see the world around me before attending the academy. Imagine getting up and going to work, laboring all day, going to the bank or store, and sitting at stop lights while looking through a soda straw. In a 'normal' environment you simply don't pay any attention to what is going on around you. This is why some people are easy targets for robberies, assaults, and thefts: They simply do not see them coming.

"After I graduated from the police academy my vision expanded to include everything that was going on around me. It was amazing to see how many people were studying me! Often these were the kind of people I did not want studying me. When they discovered that I was aware, they moved on to someone else.

"This is how we like to see new police officers leave the academy, with heightened awareness and attention to the world around them. At the end of the class I view these people as ready and confident, but still eager to move on to the next phase of training."

5. *What is your definition of a great working team when you see a class graduate from the academy?*

"I see a great core team when I see a class working together in study groups, building knowledge together, when faster runners slow down and join slower runners to encourage them, when numerous members of the class step up to take control and encourage other leaders trying to do the same, and when I see the class trying to emulate the staff in how they present themselves.

"I know we have a great team when work is getting done without supervision or direction from the staff, when there are so many people endeavoring together that there is not enough work for everyone, when I see people eager to show up for work with smiles on their faces, looking forward to another day. This is a definition of a great working team."

6. *What is your most difficult challenge in training police officers?*

"My greatest challenge is confronting the ego of that one person who believes they have what it takes and does not need the training, that all he or she needs to do is 'go through the motions.' These people take a great deal more time than others and require a healthier and more involved investment from the staff.

"If they are to succeed in the field training process, we must help them change this faulty character and form it into one that is adaptable to training. We try to accomplish this by developing structured training regimens, progress meetings, setting examples and demonstrating the cause and effect issues that can arise if structure is not adhered to. Our desire for their success makes us get them involved with the team, making them hold themselves accountable for their actions."

7. *What is your most significant win in training police officers?*

"My greatest personal satisfaction in training police officers is watching them take the oath of office, getting ready to set out on a new career, a career which I helped launch. I know this could be the start for them of a lifetime of gratification in helping others.

"As this interview for the book was progressing, I was paid a visit by one of my former recruits who said to me, 'Thank you so much for investing your time, patience, and diligence into my dream of becoming who I am right now. I would do this job for free if I could. On the days I feel less than 100%, I hear your voice telling me to get up, push harder, work smarter, show the command presence to everyone I come into contact with, and to keep my head on a swivel. Because of you, I do my best every day.'

"It is in those times that I know I have fulfilled my duties as a trainer and team builder. I cannot describe the rush I feel, the complete satisfaction and pride I experience. It drives me to do the best I can do. I believe that if you are a great supervisor, you are going to supervise great people. Every day I can't wait to go to work to see great people emerge."

Rob is a superb core team leader. He showcases what maturing group leaders should demonstrate. Let's extrapolate the characteristics.

First, as a leader, he sets initial standards of quality relationships (making the decisions about his recruits' successes) and excellence of function (the tasks that prove the truth of the relationships) by showing what is expected, not just talking about it. Great leaders tell and show. Full engagement in real life is not just discussed, it's done.

He groups his recruits into team units, treating them like the core teams they will become. Rob and his staff provide upfront examples of team empowerment, follow-through, and loyalty, explaining that lives — their lives — may depend on the degrees of cooperation they exercise. It is when the recruits are motivated on their own initiative that Rob and his staff know their investments are working.

Setting high standards of relationship and function requires correction of less than desirable behaviors and reinforcement of good ones. Both are accomplished within a framework that continually works toward desired improvements. The great team endeavors to achieve best practices because they are dedicated to long term as well as short term effects.

Determination and submission are not foreign elements on a working core team, one where loyalty to each other and the goals of the group are prevalent. Proper submission to authority is part of determination. Rob combines these values well in his statement, "We are not looking for robots, but individuals who have compassion and drive — people who are able to work with limited supervision in total confidence." You know the process of core team training is producing well when compassion and drive cooperate, and confidence is raised.

Rob's estimation of a great working team is significant. He highlights team members who offer assistance to others, take the initiative to own solutions, and showcase so much efficiency that jobs are completed with excellence. The proof is in the people who are learning to contribute because they want to, not because they have to, and are doing so because this way of operation has become part of them.

Interestingly, the greatest challenge Rob notes, is ego. An ego that tries to stonewall investment is not accountable and therefore will prove to be unreliable. It is dealt with upfront. The confrontation is not optional if the recruit with the ego is going to be part of a functioning team whose members' lives may rest upon the exercise of values that bind this group together. An over-inflated ego is replaced with cooperation that comes from proper obedience to shared principles, seen in the practices that work for the good of the whole and the people the team serves.

When great leadership has invested in the growth of the individuals on the core team, the highest satisfaction will be the success of the followers. Rehearsing the steps that lead to greater accomplishment provides the platform for producing enduring performances. Not much more needs to be said to amplify this truth than this: Leaders who build long-lasting and fruitful legacy want, more than anything else, to see their followers win — and win in a big way. Their applause lives in what their followers achieve.

Innovation Is Part of the Strategic Plan

One of the ways that finely tuned core teams rehearse and perform great customer servicing is through responsible strategic planning that allows spaces and places for innovation. Creative freedom granted to members of a core team is granted to, and earned by, those who prove that investments in people produce long-lasting and beneficial results.

The more a work cluster contributes out of health, the better the product will be in the long run. There are multiple benefits to investing in team members, and providing innovation is one of them.

Innovation from focused and dedicated people who are making great decisions about each other's successes will produce better methods, products, means of delivery, and heightened profit. Stifling innovation by not providing spaces and places for it simply doesn't make sense. If a team is committed to relational and functional growth, innovation will be encouraged.

Stated alternatively, a leader who desires greatness in customer service provision, who wants the model of what the team does on the inside to become the demonstration of what the team provides to customers on the outside, will create structures that encourage contributions from creative minds, in spite of how busy people are.

Day-to-day business is consumptive. It is a recurring challenge to operate so efficiently that dedicated spaces and places for creative problem solving are integrated into the strategic planning of the organization. The effective leader marks the dates and times for team members to engage in activities that stimulate them to greatness within everything they do.

Superior customer servicing is a by-product of responsible strategic planning. When the planning is done within a balance of relationship and function, spaces and places are made for innovation. The chart below showcases this.

Responsible Strategic Planning: Providing Spaces and Places for Innovation

---

Input and Output illustrate vibrant strategic planning.

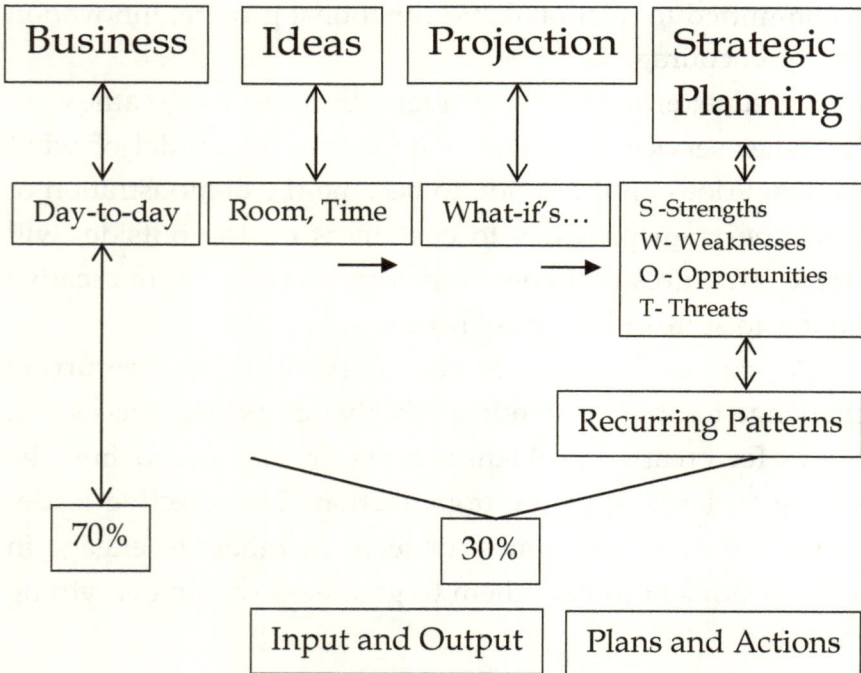

Business	Ideas	Projection	Strategic Planning
↕	↕	↕	↕
Day-to-day	Room, Time	What-if's...	S - Strengths
	→	→	W - Weaknesses
			O - Opportunities
			T - Threats

Recurring Patterns

70%   30%

Input and Output   Plans and Actions

A great core team strives to create a structure for strategic planning that provides needed spaces and places for innovation and constant input and output. Freedom in structure encourages creative minds to address issues from fresh perspectives. A day-to-day business operation may consume 70% of a team's time and energy. Set aside up to 30% for generating new ideas—give them room and time. Project "what-if's" as part of strategic planning. When a team member comes up with a great idea, check it against Strengths, Weaknesses, Opportunities, and Threats (SWOT). Set recurring patterns of input and output, plans and actions.

To summarize: The core team that wants best deliverables in customer service provision builds the staff that provides the service. They rehearse their investments in one another to provide models from which they learn and through which they grow. They encourage their members to take initiative in serving the customer. They provide spaces and places for innovation as part of their strategic plan. They know that what they rehearse among themselves equates to what they perform for the people who keep them in business—their customers.

> The proof is in the people.

Chapter 8:
Rehearsal and Performance —
A Customer Service Model

Principles are the foundations for living and working well. They must be embraced and obeyed. All of us have reserves of values upon which we can draw, and everyday workplace opportunities call on members of a core team to employ them. When the values upon which a team agrees are freely distributed and exercised, they become part of a healthy balance of relationships and functions.

The opportunity is to understand why, how, when, and to what degree to implant valued truths. There should be no reservation regarding their use. The application of values into the workplace is where true character is evidenced. If we hold to the worth of core values and express them in words, then we must consider this question: When does what we say become what we do?

Learning and applying are not the same actions. These separate but inter-related activities are sequential. A core team does well to engage in both, especially in times of challenge.

Victory in one circumstance is preparation for the next when a team has learned from their experience. Learning is a trait of developing character. Acting on what has been learned is proof that behaviors are willfully changing.

The textbook for teams who want to learn and practice the lessons they embrace is made up of their core values and their value system. Greatness appears when what they know is true is evidenced daily in what they do.

Paul's Example of Leadership

When I met with Paul for an interview for *Core Teams Work Their Principles and Practices* it became quickly apparent that this man had deep dedication to helping his workers achieve their best. Paul is the operations director for a conference center. He works with twelve employees who answer to him through three supervisors.

Paul leads by example as well as by directive. He would rather model behavior than explain it, but he does both. In fact, he adopts various methods of leadership according to the degrees of communication receptivity of each of his team members. Preferring to be less directive and more inclusive, he leads from principle, through practice. It's a strong combination. And sometimes it's difficult. Paul mentioned, "It is much easier to not care and delegate from the cuff of convenience, but leading with truth down the path of correctness becomes a habit even when it isn't easy. It is a responsibility." Well said.

Leaders who adapt their leadership forms to best relate to those who follow are growing to understand the second and third laws of the **"Twelve Laws of Understanding" (see page 207 of** *Core Teams Work***):**

- Law #2: Seek to understand how the other person thinks and communicates; use his or her language.
- Law #3: Model what I want.

Time, effort, and dedication are required to lead well, show consistency, monitor how well communication is occurring, and evaluate results. Paul uses his reserves of relationship to communicate with his team. His members not only know what he wants functionally from them, he also offers his reasons behind the directions. His desire that they understand is evidence that he wants their best. He uses his reserves unreservedly. The challenge is to work toward mutual agreement, even applying a push if necessary, while protecting and cherishing a person's dignity, to achieve best results on behalf of his people and their production.

Acquiring knowledge of how to lead in multiple situations is part of a learning experience for the whole team, and the efforts are accomplished with a firm dedication to exercising integrity. Paul states, "Integrity can only be seen when it is proved." He's right. If it isn't present and can't be seen, then a core team can dissolve within broken relationships, and its functional contributions will assuredly suffer.

Every core team goes through challenging times when relational reserves must be tapped to restore strength and renew confidence. When relationships are consistently built, then these reserves are present for use, and they should be accessed without reservation.

Leadership yearns for discovering viable ways of knowing truth and, with wisdom, applying it constantly. While it is sometimes hard to get to the truth when relationships are strained, a leader will make diligent efforts to communicate with integrity, and model, by example, this principle: Truth works.

When values are identified they become truth standards that must be ratified. They become active traits that a strong and maturing work group agrees they want to embrace and employ.

When a team decides what their values are, and what they mean, they commit to fulfilling them. The list of core values they identify, define, and ratify is a guide as well as a measurement of success or failure of their efforts to live them out. Of course, a list of values is just that—a list. A value system **(as explained in *Leadership Is*— pages 143 - 155)** is a collection of declared commitments to apply and accomplish. The **"Twelve Laws of Understanding" on page 207 of *Core Teams Work*** is a sample of a value system. A core team is encouraged to develop both a values list *and* a value system.

Values are intangibles—they cannot be bought or sold, handled, smelled, or tasted. However, each member of a working cluster knows whether they are present or absent. Intangibles produce tangibles—results that can be seen and touched, bought and sold—when utilized to their full potential.

An inventory or reservoir of values for your team to consider is below. Certainly not an exhaustive collection, it does include many principles on which many core teams agree. Whether your core team, company, organization, department, or firm has yet established its values list and accompanying definitions and applications, you are invited to review this list. While some of these words are synonymous with others, and some are used to define and describe others, you are encouraged to choose those core values that best exemplify those traits of good character you and your team want to embrace.

They are presented in alphabetical order. Which of these do you see as worthy traits that already appear or should become apparent within your group's relationships and functionality? Which of these does your team declare as its own? Which should your team adopt and implement? Which of these values will you, whether you are the leader or follower, commit to fostering within yourself and on your team?

The Core Values of the Core Team

- Accountability
- Accuracy
- Advancement
- Affirmation
- Appreciation
- Assistance
- Assurance
- Balance
- Belief
- Camaraderie
- Care
- Celebration
- Character
- Clarity

- Closure
- Commitment
- Communication
- Compassion
- Competence
- Confidence
- Connectivity
- Consideration
- Consistency
- Contemplation
- Cooperation
- Courage
- Creativity
- Decisiveness
- Dedication
- Dependability
- Desire
- Dignity
- Diversity
- Drive
- Education
- Effort
- Encouragement
- Endurance
- Engagement
- Enthusiasm
- Ethics
- Example
- Experience
- Faith
- Faithfulness
- Family
- Follow-through
- Forgiveness
- Fortitude
- Freedom
- Friendship
- Generosity
- Gentleness
- Giving
- Grace
- Gratitude
- Growth
- Happiness
- Health
- Help
- Honesty
- Honor
- Hope
- Humility
- Humor
- Inclusion
- Initiative
- Innovation
- Inquisitiveness
- Inspiration

- Integrity
- Intentionality
- Interest
- Investment
- Judgment
- Justice
- Kindness
- Knowledge
- Laughter
- Law
- Leadership
- Learning
- Legacy
- Listening
- Longevity
- Love
- Loyalty
- Maturity
- Mercy
- Morality
- Motivation
- Nurture
- Obedience
- Openness
- Patience
- Peace
- Permission
- Perseverance
- Perspective
- Planning
- Positive attitudes
- Potential
- Preparation
- Pro-activity
- Provision
- Receiving
- Recreation
- Redemption
- Refreshment
- Rehabilitation
- Relationships
- Reliability
- Resolve
- Respect
- Responsiveness
- Rest
- Restitution
- Restoration
- Results
- Reward
- Self-control
- Service
- Sharing
- Spontaneity
- Stability
- Strength

- Success
- Support
- Teaching
- Teamwork
- Tenacity
- Thanksgiving
- Truth

- Time
- Trust
- Validation
- Vision
- Wealth
- Wholeness
- Wisdom

A Value System

Twelve Laws of Understanding

1. Realize I am responsible for my own choices, not others'; that changing someone else's behavior is not my responsibility; rather, I need to change me.

2. Seek to understand how the other person thinks and communicates; use his or her language.

3. Model what I want.

4. Set realistic limits on what is acceptable behavior.

5. Impose these limits on myself, first.

6. Desire the best, but prepare for difficulty; seek creative, peaceful solutions.

7. Seek and pray for wisdom.

8. Remember, at the right times.

9. Encourage always.

10. Think first, listen most, and speak seldom.

11. Realize growth involves change, change can mean pain, and patience on the journey is a virtue.

12. Love. Establish meaningful relationships.

© 2005 by Glen Aubrey. All Rights Reserved.
www.glenaubrey.com

A leader's responsibility is to embody the principles that the core team agrees are their standards of attitude and action, to endeavor to make what is on the page become the actions that recur throughout the days. A core team member's obligation is to commit to the same thing.

Leaders and followers know that example-setting is not perfection-achieving; rather, perseverance-embracing. Members of a core team who want health and wealth commit wholeheartedly to acting on what they know is right.

Values and Relational Conflict Resolution

Conflict happens in any growth environment. Where resolution is needed to any issue involving people, product, systems, or communication, the leader and his or her team must propose solutions. A leader sets the pace and puts positive solution ideas in place for consideration.

The key, however, is for the leader to create ownership of ideas and their implementation by encouraging others on his or her team to come up with needful solutions. Sometimes this is no small task, especially when the leader is positioned as the primary idea-generator who moves and motivates the team.

One arena where applied values can emerge victorious is when members on a team have developed negative issues with one another. For issues that are relationally based, when one team member is perceived to have committed a wrong, unwise, insensitive, and unfortunate choice about another team member's success, there is a system of resolution that works well when it is employed fully.

Look at this simple diagram.

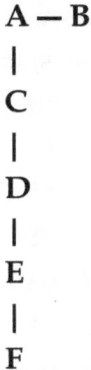

```
A — B
|
C
|
D
|
E
|
F
```

For this illustration, let's say that person A has an issue, regardless of the reason, with person B. Conflict resolution communication occurs when A goes directly to B and uses the procedures described in *Leadership Is—* **pages 103 - 108 and illustrated on page 164.**

Many times, however, what occurs is this: Instead of A going directly to B, A goes to C and "explains" the situation. Whether or not this communication is couched in "needing counsel" or "just venting," it has tremendous potential for destruction. More often than not, this communication is simply gossip.

When presented with information from A, C has some very important choices to consider. The first one to reject is to take the communication to person D, who will more than likely take it to E. Perhaps E will share it with F and so forth.

Obviously the person who is clueless when this gossip occurs is the object of all these discussions, person B.

The most valued and respected choices C should make are these:

1. C asks A if A has gone to B with the problem.
2. If the answer is "yes," then C can offer assistance if needed or requested, and if permission is obtained to do so.
3. If the answer is "no," then C has these options:
   a. C encourages or requires A to go directly to B.
   b. If A refuses to go directly to B, then C can say to A, "I'll go with you."
   c. If A refuses that offer, then C politely but firmly says, "Then this conversation is concluded."

There are management theories and mandates that say that a responsibility of any team participant is to report negative issues up without trying to solve them at the point of occurrence first. In some situations this operational paradigm may be required, notably when illegal behavior is observed or proven, in instances where disclosure of information to another party is prohibited by law, or in the interest of security or other sensitive applications.

However, for the vast majority of relationship- and issue-oriented problems, the maturity level of your core team membership, including its leadership, is shown by the willingness to take the most direct route to accomplish resolution to an issue that must be addressed, where the people who own the problem initially own the responsibility of solving it.

Values and Transfer of Ownership

Values-driven and connecting leaders encourage solution thinking (relational decisions) and acting (corroborating functions) on the part of their teams for any issues that must be addressed. Sharing the processes of solution provision is part of the transfer of ownership. Transfer of ownership is not abdication; rather, it is allowing an ownership process to be done correctly, with correct intent, ultimate respect, and honor.

To include the team in solution creation and implementation, leaders often ask thought-provoking questions that cannot be answered "yes" or "no." These are "what if..." and "how could..." or "what kind of solutions would you recommend?" questions.

For example:

1. How could we accomplish this action better?
2. What systems could we employ that would help us achieve a stronger bottom line?
3. What do you recommend?
4. What is your opinion?
5. What are our alternatives?
6. What if we considered another plan?
7. How could we think about this differently?
8. What has your research revealed?
9. Why are you convinced that this proposal will, or will not, work?
10. What results should we anticipate, when, and who should know?

11. What is your solution?

12. When may we receive your plan for solution provision?

When a core team adheres to its values it cooperates to create and implement solutions. Healthy and vibrant core group clusters enjoy solving problems through transferred ownership, not dependent on their leader to be the exclusive originator of good ideas or plans. When all participate to provide solutions because they agree on principle, ownership is shared.

A leader knows he or she has transferred ownership when the solutions come from, and are implemented by, the core team. A core team knows it has transferred the ownership of solution provision toward the highest good when no member cares who gets the credit for the great idea, and no member dwells on who should receive the blame if an idea does not come to fruition or proves to be unworkable.

A core team leader who wants to challenge his or her team participants toward more aggressive innovation may choose to present an idea for consideration that he or she is pretty sure won't work, telling the team that this is exactly what is occurring. Far from manipulation, this is truth-telling that stimulates those who wish to contribute alternative and improved processes, to do so. In other words, if the idea the leader is proposing proves to be inadequate, who will rise to the occasion to offer a superior substitute?

Further, a core team leader who is dedicated to creating frameworks in which core team members can grow may already have the correct or best solution in mind, but may not present it outright, preferring instead to provide open atmospheres and innovative opportunities for new thinking on the part of team members. Directives, where a solution is imposed from above, may not be nearly as effective as including others in resolution discussions—so the ideas become theirs. People who want to be a part of a solution enjoy the process, if they're in it.

It may be that the leader has had a solution design in mind from the beginning, but through positive team discourse the idea becomes one that the followers invent. When this occurs, the leader who is committed to his or her team's successes congratulates the solution providers, moves ahead on making the best decisions and, if he or she is secure, doesn't need to reveal that the chosen idea was in the mind of the leader first. In fact, it's far better if the leader doesn't play his or her hand in this way. A well-grounded and motivating person who wants the best for the team will be quite content to remain silent and let others enjoy their victories.

Freedom to openly share responsible idea creation does not come from dysfunctional people who do not trust each other. In fact, true freedom of interchanging fresh thoughts and perspectives only comes from work clusters that willfully trust, congratulate, and are honest in assessment, while protecting each other's dignity. Enhanced relationships strengthen a team's functions.

When to intervene, or not, is a choice a leader makes on the basis of relational reserves, not reservations born of misguided motives, manipulation, intimidation, or insecurity. If you are the leader, ask yourself if you hold too tightly to your own agendas, excluding creativity and contributions of others on your team. If you do, then consider why. A leader who hordes is not a leader who helps. A leader who prevents others from achieving is not the leader who produces greater people. A leader who restrains followers and inhibits personal and organizational growth is not the leader who cares. A leader who pushes others out of the way as a matter of convenience is not the leader who loves.

Great leaders and willing followers apply principles upon which they agree through transferring ownership and sharing responsibility. Oh, by the way, they produce enhanced products and profits, too.

> When all participate to provide solutions because they agree on principle, ownership is shared.

The Reservoir of Values

Core teams who have identified their values, and who strive to live within their agreed value system treat their reservoir of values as both a place to draw from and a reserve to add to. How the reservoir is filled up and how its contents are utilized come from good and proper core team decision-making.

Benefits flow from this reservoir without reservation when the reserves are freely invested in the welfare (right standing) of the people on the team. Distributing them without inhibition among the team's membership demonstrates a team's relational strength.

On a great team, values are enhanced when they are freely employed. Cooperative engagement is composed of giving and receiving, and everyone shares in the positive results.

Values actively employed produce multiple wins. When the reserves are let loose to do their good deeds, then the true characters of the people who participate are readily seen. What they believe and are committed to, are evidenced in real life engagements.

Here are some noteworthy examples:

1. Appropriate information sharing, where it can be shown that its distribution causes another's work contributions to become more effective
2. Unmitigated truth
3. Creative problem-solving
4. Ownership of responsibility
5. Mutual respect
6. Courtesy
7. Operational efficiency
8. Communication loop closure
9. Facing difficult situations upfront

10. Obtaining permission for expanding networks of communication
11. Following through and fulfilling promises
12. Production excellence

Values are not withheld when they represent shared and agreed principles. Values can't be used up. A core team dedicated to more than just words on paper assures that the contents of their reservoir are intentionally distributed among its membership and those the core team serves. The return on this investment will be evidenced in exponential benefits for all recipients. This team's reservoir is never empty.

Chapter 9:
You Can Bank On It

The Story of Steve Annis and His Apprentice:
The Investors

Steve Annis is the Executive Vice President and Chief Financial Officer of a reginal financial services organization. Additionally, he leads community outreach groups where people development is a prime objective. He is also a good friend.

He and another representative within the financial services company participated in one of the leadership development training programs of Creative Team Resources Group, Inc. (www.ctrg.com). They achieved outstanding results through the process.

Steve graciously granted an interview for *Core Teams Work Their Principles and Practices*. My questions focused on the major reasons why great core teams work well, accenting duplication and the expectations of quality returns on investments.

His interview follows.

1. *Core teams have become part of the structure and systems of your financial institution. What kinds of differences in staff communication and heightened business effectiveness do you see when these teams work well?*

   "When our teams are working well, there is an improvement in the level of communication between team members as well as between various teams. Improved communication, in turn, results in improved job performance, improved individual job satisfaction, and improved customer satisfaction. One of our corporate culture goals is to eliminate the tendency of employees to claim 'That's not my job' or 'That's not my problem.' When core teams are working properly, those tendencies disappear. What replaces them is ownership of jobs and fulfillment of responsibility. The result is that our customers are cared for, no matter who is serving them."

2. *What are some of the challenges that your core teams face?*

   "With our industry changing so rapidly, combined with a seemingly ever-increasing load of government regulations and oversight, it is very easy to get so inwardly-focused that we can lose sight of the big picture of who we are and why we do what we do. As the old saying goes, 'It's hard to remember that your objective is to drain the swamp when you are up to your ears in alligators.' Sometimes it just seems like the alligators are gaining on us. And, of course, when the alligators are gaining, it is extremely easy to put aside that which will advance team understanding, cohesion, and effort in favor of expediting one-on-one alligator extermination. The real challenge for me is to recognize that doing that which will advance the health and functioning of our core teams is of far greater importance over the long term than stopping one alligator — even a really big, ugly one. When core teams work well they face challenges with an eye on prioritizing what is really important against that which isn't, and dealing with the most important items appropriately."

3. *How does conflict resolution occur within and on behalf of the core teams?*

"Conflicts are going to naturally arise in any work environment. When we have our core teams functioning properly, conflicts within the teams tend to be handled by the team members, within the core teams, without the need for management intervention. When conflicts arise between the core teams, the focus for the team leaders is to attempt to resolve those conflicts between themselves, on behalf of their respective teams, without escalation. If management intervention is required, the arbitration and resolution of inter-team conflicts flows more easily and resolution is typically more readily achieved from the strong relationships and desires expressed by leaders committed to each other's success."

4. *What are some personal and core team personnel investment "wins" that you have experienced as you have put core team principles and practices into place at your organization?*

"I have identified one individual who currently works for me as the person most likely to be my replacement when I retire in a few years. Being able to embark on a journey of discovery with him, learning and applying the concepts of 'investment leadership' has been an outstanding experience. Through my investment in this individual, I am seeing my legacy in the ongoing success of this company actually manifesting itself before my eyes. In turn, he and I have identified four other people within our organization who are either current department heads or are clearly on a fast track to becoming department heads. We are beginning to mentor and invest in these people through regular meetings and study of core team investment leadership concepts. These individuals are learning and applying these principles in their respective areas of responsibility. The ultimate impact on our organization, I believe, will be incredible."

Return on Investment (ROI):

Efforts spent to help promote a follower's success will pay multiple dividends in the long run if the investments are well-placed. In *Leadership Is—* several factors of the processes of building legacy are covered. You are invited and encouraged to read and review **Chapters 8, 9, and 10** of this leadership legacy book.

ROI is a tangible demonstration of a lot of hard work, confidence, and trust. Interestingly, in leadership and core team development, the ROI is not just a product seen at the end, or upon review of an action's conclusion; rather, this return is evidenced as part of the process of growth *throughout* the engagement.

Investment in people matures the participants *while* they engage in the activity, so the benefits are multiple. This trait is the truth to which Steve is referring in his interview when he says, "Through my investment in this individual, I am seeing my legacy in the ongoing success of this company actually manifesting itself before my eyes." I have observed Steve and his highly qualified apprentice during this process, and I have met the four people into whom Steve and this other gentlemen are investing. Attending a meeting with all six of them, I was pleasantly and gratifyingly amazed, again, at how transferable core team investments are.

Simply put, when a core team invests in its people, the growth is not under the radar; it is upfront and openly celebrated. It produces enhanced work products along with improved and maturing people. What is needed in the understanding of the procedure is a reminder and re-commitment to this truth: the process is more important than the end result.

Look around where you see teams functioning from a relationship- and values-driven model, and you will see maturity occurring and recurring. There really is no end to this healthy interaction — it feeds (nourishes) those who are part of the activity, continually.

Let's state this another way: If you are the leader, and you are striving to invest in the people on your team, but you are not seeing results in behavioral changes before your eyes, there are problems — maybe big ones — and you need to know about them.

A few of them may be represented here:

1. You have people on your team who do not want you to lead, or who do not respect your leadership.
2. You have followers who do not want to mature.
3. The "Code of Achievement" (values, vision, mission and message) may be unknown.
4. You have a team with members who do not adhere to the "Code of Achievement" if it is known.
5. You have people on your team who are more interested in turf protection than they are cooperation.
6. You have people on your team who are jealous of one another's successes.
7. You have people who are trying to undercut one another.
8. You have people on your team who are telling you through their words and deeds that they do not desire to remain as contributing members.

9. You have people who are not engaged in truth-telling and are hiding behind their own insecurities or inadequacies.
10. You have people who may be functional, but clearly are not relational (are not making decisions about other people's success).
11. You have people who do not honor the value of the company's or their own personal resources.
12. You don't have a core team in the model of *Core Teams Work Their Principles and Practices.*

A return on investment from work activities will be seen whenever a group comes together for the right reasons and exercises right behaviors. Their processes showcase their confidence in their outcomes.

1. A solid team declares its purposes, and establishes authority and accountability.
2. The team communicates, sets priorities, assigns tasks, engages its people, owns responsibilities, fulfills jobs well, sees its members mature, and realizes profits.

A great team expects exceptional returns from their quality decisions and actions. None of these are hidden or assumed.

Upon a firm, resolute declaration and agreement of values, vision, mission, and message, a great core team embraces its principles and demonstrates them in practice through investing in its people. They produce enhanced and more excellent products, and enjoy the journey even when conflicts arise. Evidence proves that this group really is a core team.

If a work cluster wants quantitative and long lasting returns they will engage in quality investment in its personnel. One of the most positive means of investing well is treating each other with courtesy.

Courtesy

Courtesy is a tell-tale sign of health on a great core team, or within any relationship for that matter. Let's define this very important trait of holistic behavior. "Courtesy" is the willing attitude and corresponding action to create a place and space for another person's contributions, setting aside personal agendas for his or her benefit.

If you notice courtesy on a team you likely are witnessing a group who has validated its values, vision, mission, and message. On this team you will witness behaviors like:

1. Showing up for work on time or early
2. Listening without interrupting
3. Desires to go beyond surface expectations
4. Avoidance of gossip
5. Truth
6. Integrity
7. Declaration of values, vision, mission and message
8. Seeking great communication as a matter of course
9. Pro-active problem resolution
10. No whining
11. Encouragement
12. Faithfulness to duty
13. Respect

14. Honor
15. Love
16. Happiness (a joyful environment)
17. Accountable autonomy, where a person given a job fulfills it whether or not anyone is looking
18. More than sufficient preparation for a task, especially where another's contributions depend on it
19. Anticipation of need
20. Fulfillment of obligation, in advance of due date
21. Initiative
22. Industry
23. Goodwill
24. Interest in the goals of the team
25. Valuing contributions of each member and showing appreciation, regardless of status, position, title, or tenure
26. Treasuring company resources and exercising responsible stewardship **(see *Industrial Strength Solutions*, page 105)**
27. Excellence of provision
28. Competence and desires to grow, learn, and contribute more
29. Building up team members in front of peers and superiors
30. Affirmations
31. Celebrations

*Questions for your team: How often do we see courtesy
exercised at our workplace? What are recent evidences of
courtesy in action? What are incidents that clearly show a lack
of courtesy?*

The courses of daily activities, whether pleasant or difficult, are the proving grounds of courtesy. Active courtesy in day-to-day work environments is a true life illustration of quality relationships and functions. Teams who exercise courtesy produce solid returns on their investments — in their processes, with their people, for their benefit.

Chapter 10
Core Issues for Core Teams

Creative Team Resources Group has identified twenty-one core issues that core teams repeatedly encounter. Regardless of the nature of the organization, scope of its products, delivery mechanisms, customer or vendor relationships, whether for-profit, not-for-profit, large, small, public- or private-sector, the following topics are high priority items. Each must be examined and acted upon by any group who wants to flourish.

Growth is measured in how well these issues are identified and articulated, and by how their challenges and opportunities are proactively addressed. You and your team are encouraged to consider them.

They are presented alphabetically as a list, then with commentary where each issue is described. Issues are then cross-referenced.

Cross-reference page numbers for *Leadership Is —* and *Industrial Strength Solutions* are compiled from the 2012 versions of both books. Cross-reference page numbers for *Core Teams Work* are compiled from the 2019 version.

21 Core Issues for Core Teams

Accountability
Behavioral change
Commitments that stand
Communication
Conflict resolution
Consistent follow-through
Desires and decisions to help others succeed
Enlarged "global" awareness
Evaluation methods
Excellence in personal and team task completion,
doing jobs right, and finishing well
Expanded service population numbers
Healthy relationships
Increased productivity
Increased profits
Modeling
Performance
Problem solving and solution-based thinking
Reward systems
Strength and solidarity in crises
Transfer of ownership
Trust

21 Core Issues Commentary and Cross-References

1. *Accountability*

"Consider it done" is one of the genuinely expressed phrases I enjoy saying and hearing. When that phrase is combined with reliable action, the person who has fulfilled a responsibility is one on whom the core team can count. If accountability is what a team really wants, it is modeled from its leadership to its followers before it is required by leadership from those who follow. Coupled with authority, accountability is a staple of a strong and maturing group. Where authority is a relationship defined, accountability is functional proof that the relationship is true. (*Leadership Is —*, **pages 54 - 58, 62 - 71, 164 - 166;** *Industrial Strength Solutions*, **pages 102, 219 - 221;** *Core Teams Work*, **pages 19 - 24, 27, 36, 53, 63 -106, 119, 122, 127 - 133, 141 – 155, 157 - 164, 168 - 179.)**

2. *Behavioral change*

Desire, decision, and dedication are required when a person considers changing his or her behavior to achieve more positive results. Behaviors are choices, and desires to alter them can originate from many sources. The receptivity to ideology and values, with which the person agrees, is one source. Another is when new views become true views. These may cause reconsideration of foundations of thinking and acting. Open minds embrace opportunities to learn and apply principles into daily life. In this attitude of receptivity, a person and a core team weigh the merits of what they learn against the core values they share. If a desired result equates to a change in behavior, and the means and ends do not violate the values they hold, a person or a team will alter behaviors to align with new information. Remember, communication is not complete or as effective as it could be, and learning becomes living only when behaviors change. (*Leadership Is —*, **pages 20, 89 – 92, 102, 107, 118, 148, 153, 237;** *Industrial Strength Solutions*, **pages 232 - 235, 260, 281, 284, 337;** *Core Teams Work*, **pages 19, 24, 26, 42, 64 - 108, 147, 161 - 173, 179, 181, 188, 193, 199 - 201, 207, 211, 214 - 216.**)

3. *Commitments that stand*

Loyalty is tried and tested in times of stress. Loyalty is a demonstration of faithfulness. Faithfulness comes from unwavering commitment. Commitments that stand transcend and sometimes change the circumstances that may war against their will. A core team that stays committed to task fulfillment, honoring time, target, and treasure, as well as the people within its group, is one that learns and applies the lessons of building confidence and assurance through whatever they encounter. A committed individual is the one on whom the work group can depend, regardless of circumstances. A mixture of these people comprises a great core team. (*Leadership Is —*, **pages 42, 47, 62, 81, 85, 87, 99, 106, 114,**

118, 121, 136, 173, 178, 196, 225, 237; *Industrial Strength Solutions,* **pages 17 - 19, 32 - 34, 45, 52, 64 - 72, 79, 93 - 103, 113 - 115, 147, 162, 177, 182 - 188, 193, 198, 208 - 213, 216 -223, 225 - 235, 240 - 244, 261, 267, 284 - 287;** *Core Teams Work,* **pages 19 - 21, 49, 53, 59 - 65, 99 - 111, 119 - 122, 127, 130 - 134, 140, 155, 164, 175, 202 - 204, 222.)**

4. *Communication*

The desire for consistent and efficient, open and honest exchange of ideas is the topic that nearly always tops the list of vital issues. Perhaps the single most important aspect of communication is that its effectiveness is revealed in improved behaviors. Communication that is information-sharing only may be profitable to a point. Communication that lasts, however, will cause people to act, to put decisions expressed in words into practices of works. (*Leadership Is —,* **pages 20, 41, 69, 73, 77, 78, 88, 100 – 103, 105 - 108, 111 - 119, 133, 147, 164, 179, 188 - 191, 198, 209, 224, 226, 228, 236, 246;** *Industrial Strength Solutions,* **pages 18, 24, 34, 36, 97, 111 - 115, 182 - 196, 203 - 206, 210, 212, 219 - 223, 229 - 235, 261;** *Core Teams Work,* **pages 59 - 65, 79, 83, 85 - 89, 123 - 130, 135 - 152, 179, 185, 201 – 204, 207 - 223.)**

5. *Conflict resolution*

Expect conflict to be a part of the human experience. Seen in work, family, social settings, or any environment where people interact, conflict is probable where more than one person is present. Because participants on a core team are not robots, they will sometimes oppose each other relationally or functionally. In fact, some of the greatest solution provision may originate from challenging interchanges. Handle them well. Conflict that divides, casts negative aspersions, builds barricades to communication, and destroys healthy relationships is generally discord that is not being dealt with appropriately or in a timely manner. If a team wants to continue to grow through trying experiences, it will find and utilize proven methods to resolve conflicts, and mature each other through the process. Open lines of communication are required, as is complete honesty and adherence to shared values. **(*Leadership Is —*, pages 41, 73, 103 - 108, 119; *Industrial Strength Solutions*, pages 136, 187, 194, 212, 216 - 222, 261, 283; *Core Teams Work*, pages 51 - 53, 112, 119, 129 - 133, 140, 161, 172 - 174, 208 - 210, 219, 223 - 226.)**

6. *Consistent follow-through*

Stability, accountability, and reliability are three co-existent traits of healthy core teams who follow through to faithfully complete their duties. **From *Leadership Is —*, page 62:** "Stability is shown when the relational decisions toward being a person of trust and truth are given context and illustration in outward demonstration in dealings with others. Accountability is stability in duplicative action; it is ongoing and able to be repeated." Reliability, as described in ***Core Teams Work***, "…describes reliance on the *ability* of the person tasked to perform a job." A team who follows through is one that consistently attends to the details of task accomplishment and communication loop closure, not permitting essential elements of a transaction or process to fall through the cracks. The team fulfills their obligations well because their competencies match their roles and responsibilities. (*Leadership Is —*, **pages 39, 80, 99, 164, 191, 238 - 240;** *Industrial Strength Solutions*, **pages 47, 94 - 99, 261, 280 - 287;** *Core Teams Work*, **pages 20 - 24, 47 - 50, 64 - 71, 110, 119, 128 - 133, 152, 158, 177 - 179, 200 - 203.**)

7. *Desires and decisions to help others succeed*

Part of a strong relationship (the decision about someone else's success) is the evidence of the desire to help core team members achieve their goals. **As noted in** *Leadership Is —*, **page 16:** "Success in leadership achievement is defined as seeing another person fulfill their dreams and goals with the leader's teaching, modeling, encouragement, and support." Making positive decisions about a person's success does not mean that the one making the decisions owns the successes of the other person. It means that an atmosphere of assistance and encouragement is created by the one who cares for the other. In this environment, training and tools are provided, and affirmation and celebration are commonplace. Desires to help others win are openly expressed, never assumed. These traits are characteristics of a solid team and become evident to the

people it serves. (*Leadership Is—*, pages 21 - 24, 41, 54,
62 - 64, 69, 80 - 85, 87 - 92, 99, 105 - 108, 122 - 124,
128 - 132, 143 - 155, 165 - 171, 173 - 176, 177 - 183, 187, 197,
198 - 204, 208 - 210, 228, 237 - 240; *Industrial Strength
Solutions*, pages 28, 36 - 46, 59 - 72, 76 - 87, 90 - 115,
125 - 129, 135 - 144, 161, 174 - 198, 203 - 223, 227, 240 - 261,
264, 274 - 276, 284 - 287; *Core Teams Work*, pages 15 - 24,
30, 35 - 53, 65 - 71, 76 - 114, 127 - 133, 140 - 155, 159 - 173,
192 - 194, 172 - 179, 220 - 226.)

8. *Enlarged "global" awareness*
Isolationism, seen in silos and stovepipes, is not allowed
on a core team operating within a business life
investment model. No one stands alone in a working
cluster that works together. Integrated mixtures of
people who provide solutions enjoy opportunities of
combining strengths in open atmospheres of creative
innovation. Rugged individualism is not sacrificed in
these engagements; it is honored and promoted as
persons are encouraged to be their best in cooperation
with, and promotion of, the rest of the team. No one
hides or hibernates on a producing core team. Within
vitalized atmospheres of production exists a growing
recognition of the importance of individual contributions
in relation to the whole. Core teams appreciate the added
value of each person and honor what each member
brings to the group. (*Leadership Is—*, pages 21 - 29,
54 - 58, 62 - 64, 73 - 80, 85 - 92, 103 - 108, 111 - 119, 123,
124, 128 - 138, 141 - 143, 146 - 155, 176 - 183, 187 - 190,

192 - 204, 208 - 210, 220 - 230; *Industrial Strength Solutions*, pages 23 - 46, 61 - 72, 76 - 81, 94 - 106, 135 - 144, 154 - 198, 248 - 261, 272 - 276, 278 - 287; *Core Teams Work*, pages 29, 32 - 37, 50 - 53, 58 - 71, 91 - 94, 99 - 106, 121 - 124, 129, 135 - 155, 161 - 165, 173 - 179, 186 - 197, 219 - 226.)

9. *Evaluation methods*

Consistent and appropriate evaluation is germane to the activities of the team who wants success from the beginning of a task through its conclusion. As the prospect for any undertaking is considered, it is thoroughly surveyed, to assure that moving forward is the right decision. While procedures are ongoing, mid-course evaluations are often necessary. When projects are completed, the degrees of their success or failure are weighed. Measurements tell the team what to keep, what to discard, what to accent, and what to diminish. Also a work group's relational behaviors are appraised, and this activity is welcomed by the members who want to live and contribute in an environment of truth. Functional goals accomplished in cooperation with expanding relational strength call for evaluations that inform the team members that their people are growing simultaneously with their output. (*Leadership Is —*, pages 43, 58, 73, 105 - 108, 116, 119, 121 - 124, 234 - 237, 246; *Industrial Strength Solutions*, pages 45, 157 - 166, 196, 234, 255, 262, 285; *Core Teams Work*, pages 38 - 50,

58 - 71, 80, 83 - 87, 97 - 99, 114 – 117, 148 - 152, 166 - 171, 194 - 200.)

10. *Excellence in personal and team task completion, doing jobs right, and finishing well*

One of the proven examples that a core team is vibrant is that it wants to measure progress in specified timelines. Time sensitive evaluations that clearly demonstrate excellence, or the lack of it, are welcomed. Excellence for a team rises from desires to succeed on the parts of its individuals. Excellence and mediocrity have no allegiance to each other and cannot coexist. Part of excellence is not only completing tasks, but finishing well, **as explained in** *Leadership Is —* **,** where leaders teach followers to do even greater works than the leaders have done. Excellence is not automatic. Achieving it takes consistency, dedication, and hard work. Great core teams produce excellence and build enduring legacies because their desires to do so are parts of fulfilling their values, vision, mission, and message. **(***Leadership Is —* **, pages 24, 34, 77, 89 - 92, 100, 111, 129 - 131, 141 - 143, 169 - 171, 177, 182, 194 - 196, 204, 213 - 218, 220 - 230, 237 - 241, 245 - 249;** *Industrial Strength Solutions* **, pages 17 - 19, 32, 55 - 64, 81 - 87, 100 - 106, 108 - 115, 133 - 144, 149 - 156, 163 - 166, 172, 187 - 196, 215 - 223, 228 - 235, 249 - 261, 266 - 273, 281 - 287;** *Core Teams Work* **, pages 19 - 24, 41, 50 - 53, 62 - 65, 74 - 117, 122 - 124, 127 - 133, 153 - 155, 161, 165 - 173, 191 - 193, 216, 224 - 226.)**

11. Expanded service population numbers

A solid core team wants more. They desire increased maturity, potential, production, and profit. "Expanded service population numbers" is simply another expression for additional customers, heightened sales, increased business, and augmented bottom line figures. A team's proving ground of success begins, and then resides, in the intangible decisions they make. The team's tangible results, their living proofs of quality decisions, are seen in the numbers they achieve. (*Leadership Is*—, **pages 21, 25, 34 - 38, 39, 42 - 44, 56 - 58, 64, 73 - 76, 82, 105 - 108, 166 - 169, 173 - 175, 216 - 218, 251;** *Industrial Strength Solutions,* **pages 24, 36, 72, 90 - 94, 100 - 104, 136 - 144, 149 - 156, 168, 176 - 196, 209, 221, 228, 243, 248, 285;** *Core Teams Work,* **pages 30, 35 - 37, 46 - 50, 58 - 65, 85 - 88, 124, 135, 175 - 177, 181 - 197, 203, 214 - 216, 223.**)

12. Healthy relationships

Decisions about someone else's success foster healthy relational foundations. Decisions that promote another person's failure are also seeds of relationships, although undesirable ones. If a team desires healthy relationships, it will consistently remind its people that great decisions come first and best actions follow. Disease-free relationships originate from positive decisions; sick ones originate from decisions to tear other persons down. A work environment is one of many obvious places where relationships are integrated into the day-to-day experiences of each contributor. These decisions bear lasting fruits, good or bad. (*Leadership Is —*, **pages 18 - 20, 21 - 27, 41 - 44, 80 - 82, 87, 89 - 92, 99, 100 - 108, 112 - 119, 121 - 124, 129, 131 - 138, 145, 148 - 152, 164, 171 - 176, 180 - 183, 187, 195 - 201, 208, 228, 238;** *Industrial Strength Solutions*, **pages 21, 27 - 46, 59 - 72, 77 - 80, 90 - 108, 132, 135 - 144, 156, 174 - 182, 222, 250 - 255, 260, 264, 272 - 276, 281 - 287;** *Core Teams Work*, **pages 19 - 24, 42, 61 - 71, 96 - 106, 112 - 117, 135 - 155, 162 - 173, 181 - 186, 194 - 197, 218 - 224.)**

13. Increased productivity

Productivity can be measured, it is goal-oriented, it yearns to be evaluated, and it is time sensitive. Increasing it is part of the insatiable desire to look for and operate in better ways. Great core teams do not settle for complacency nor dwell in laziness. They don't remain on plateaus—they reach for higher vistas. Gathering and evaluating production goals and numbers reveal marked and tangible results from the efforts a hard working team expends. Their efforts produce lasting rewards. (*Leadership Is —*, **pages 23 - 29, 34 - 46, 111, 129, 141 - 143, 149, 180 - 183, 195 - 204, 213 – 218, 230;** *Industrial Strength Solutions*, **pages 17 - 28, 30 - 34, 74 – 87, 125 - 129, 132, 140 - 144, 156 - 195, 204, 206, 207 - 213, 216 - 223, 225 - 235, 250 - 257;** *Core Teams Work*, **pages 20 - 24, 35 – 50, 61 - 71, 86 – 108, 115, 119 – 133, 136 - 151, 165, 183 - 197.)**

14. Increased profits

The core team model illustrated in *Core Teams Work Their Principles and Practices,* defined in *Industrial Strength Solutions,* and described in the leader-follower relationships in *Leadership Is —,* is one that embraces financial responsibility. Part of a core team commitment to fiscal well-being is the acquisition of profit, defined as an amount in excess of the cost of doing business that can be used for expansion, investment, gifting, and contingency. Profits are not optional if a team is going to succeed. A great core team looks for the most value-driven methods to achieve and receive all the legitimate profits it can. **(*Leadership Is —,* pages 56 - 58, 111 - 119, 166 - 169, 220 - 230; *Industrial Strength Solutions,* pages 23 - 28, 110 - 115, 194, 228, 266; *Core Teams Work,* pages 35 - 50, 87 - 88, 135 - 137, 149, 177 - 179, 184 - 186, 194 - 197, 206, 213 - 216, 221 - 224.)**

15. Modeling

In the "Twelve Laws of Understanding," Law #3 states, "Model what I want." The practice of modeling is closely related to accountability. It stems from the truth that a leader will exercise accountability *to* a follower before requiring accountability *from* the follower. Core teams understand that required behavior must begin with desired behavior based on agreed and shared core values. The people of the team endeavor to erase distances between relationships and the functions that prove them. Modeling is an illustration of the cooperation between the two. It is central, not to achieving a goal of perfection, but to making progress on a path of perseverance toward what is truly desired. A model, as **described in** *Leadership Is* —, "...is a living entity, whom in character and condition illustrates the cause and actualization of relationships; where participants willingly decide and adopt principles and corroborating actions in environments they create, that foster consistency, thrive on integrity, earnestly seek excellence, and duplicate their effectiveness over time by investing in others of like passion, so that the product of the original is greater than the original itself." The act of modeling is the pathway to duplication and the creation of legacies that endure. **(*Leadership Is* —, pages 15 – 20, 26, 29, 41 - 44, 54 - 59, 77 - 83, 89 - 92, 100, 121 - 124, 129 - 132, 142 - 155, 198 - 204, 217, 223 - 228, 237 - 241, 252, 253; *Industrial Strength Solutions*, pages 21 - 28, 55 - 64, 70, 100 - 103, 133, 166, 186, 235 - 244, 252 - 255, 272, 278 - 287; *Core Teams Work*, pages 18 - 24, 30, 42 - 46, 73 - 117, 133, 159, 173 - 197, 207, 217, 222.)**

16. Performance

The bottom line will always be a marker of success or failure. It should be. Performance is all about obtaining verifiable results. To achieve best-deliverables a team must perform well. Excluding excuses and eliminating mediocrity, a performance-dedicated team contributes from relational strengths as well as functional competencies. Team members are active, engaged, and productive because they *want* to contribute in these ways, building each other up as performance processes unfold. **(***Leadership Is***—, pages 14, 22, 35 - 38, 141 - 155, 198 - 204, 228 - 230;** *Industrial Strength Solutions***, pages 40, 44, 80 - 87, 108 - 148, 226, 267 - 277, 282 - 287;** *Core Teams Work***, pages 22, 26 - 28, 32, 35 - 50, 58, 61 - 65, 81 - 87, 95 - 117, 133, 135 - 137, 143 - 152, 157 - 173, 175 - 179, 202, 208 - 216.)**

17. *Problem solving and solution-based thinking*

Industrial Strength Solutions points up the unique differences between whining and winning, indecision and initiative, circumstances and character, imbalance and balance. People who are problem solvers think and act from positions of strength because they are committed to improvement. You know you have a greatness-empowered core team when the members see challenges as opportunities and confront negatives with positives. Productive problem-solving begins with attitude. Solution-based thinking originates from strong character committed to overcoming obstacles and learning through difficulty. Start with a can-do attitude and best-practices follow. **(***Leadership Is***—, pages 28, 73 - 120, 122, 141 - 185;** *Industrial Strength Solutions***, pages 20 - 28, 37 - 41, 55 - 87, 141, 147, 199 - 223;** *Core Teams Work***, pages 21 - 27, 61 - 65, 69 - 71, 113 - 117, 127 - 130, 141 - 143, 159, 161, 195, 202, 208 - 226.)**

18. Reward systems

Systems of payments align with a team's action and the wealth it produces. Tangible rewards do not exclude intangible expressions of appreciation; rather, they validate each other and are given cooperatively. The principle is this: When a team succeeds, its successes are shared. Commensurate reward systems are true reflections of task fulfillment, proceeding from relational commitment. The design or redesign of any system of reward reflects the true context and content of the group's composition and output. **(*Leadership Is —*, pages 15, 34, 42 - 50, 63, 69, 74 - 78, 80 - 82, 105 - 108, 167 - 176, 216, 251; *Industrial Strength Solutions*, pages 71, 90 - 100, 102, 107, 135 - 140, 169 - 198, 221, 243, 261 - 254, 266, 271 - 276, 285 - 287; *Core Teams Work*, pages 21 - 23, 35 - 53, 63, 86 - 91, 146 - 151, 162, 169 - 171, 177 - 179, 184 - 186, 203, 226.)**

19. Strength and solidarity in crises

When tough times come — and they always will — it is then that a core team's true character is seen. Crises don't produce strength; instead, they reveal it. Endless numbers of stories abound of people who, in a moment of time and responding to immediate need, rise to meet an occasion and accomplish great feats. They are labeled as heroes for doing so. Heroism does not form in the time of turmoil; it is revealed in the trying moments because character has already been honed, perhaps prepared "for such a time as this." A work group who is made up of people unreservedly committed to core principles, withstands trials, temptations, tests, and torments of challenging business environments. A values-driven operational team grows stronger through misadventure, maturing for coming rounds of opportunity, contributing out of solid character, regardless. (*Leadership Is —*, **pages 38 - 41, 69, 82, 88 - 92, 115, 136, 150, 169 - 171, 175, 187, 195 - 198, 220 - 230, 237 - 241;** *Industrial Strength Solutions*, **pages 20 - 28, 30, 35 - 46, 52 - 54, 63 - 87, 93 - 106, 110 - 115, 117 - 143, 149 - 161, 203 - 221, 232, 240, 248, 251, 257 - 264, 270, 273, 281 - 287, 337 - 340;** *Core Teams Work*, **pages 15 - 17, 19 - 27, 61 - 65, 95 - 117, 119 - 133, 161, 172 - 179, 184 - 197, 199 - 216.)**

20. Transfer of ownership

A highly functional core team demonstrates dedication and cooperation as roles are fulfilled. When a person accepts the opportunity of an engagement, agrees to provide a solution to a problematic issue, or decides to become the follower into whom a leader can invest, then that person acquires the responsibility for completion of the transaction. Transferred ownership originates from shared decisions about each other's success. It is concluded when assignments are framed by adherence to values, formed through assent to duty, and finished by accomplishing tasks. A maturing core team understands that when ownership of any operation is transferred, the one who accepts and completes the job has made a great decision about the success of the team and the person who assigned the role. Transfer of ownership recurs consistently on core teams that strive to grow their people, help them produce excellence, and see them finish well. (*Leadership Is —*, pages 14, 16, 19 - 29, 38 - 41, 73 - 120, 146 - 165, 169 - 176, 189 - 204, 213 - 218, 237 - 241, 245 - 249; *Industrial Strength Solutions*, pages 17 - 28, 33 - 35, 37 - 46, 60, 64 - 72, 94 - 106, 123 - 129, 133, 145, 163 - 195, 203 - 223, 245 - 255; *Core Teams Work*, pages 57, 67 - 71, 77 - 87, 175, 177 - 179, 181 - 197, 208 - 216.)

21. *Trust*

Trust is the "T" of Core Team. Trust is unearned and granted when a relationship begins, and it is earned and proven as that relationship extends. Earned trust proves the validity of the relationships from which it comes and to which it contributes. A team exists in balance of good decisions and accompanying functional contributions when trust is present and active. It can't be bought or sold, but it is the foundation of all transactions which compose buying and selling. It is at the heart of a great business core team and a central core value. (*Leadership Is —*, pages 17, 25, 43 - 46, 62 - 64, 80 - 82, 87, 105 - 108, 148, 164 - 171, 198 - 204, 216 - 230, 233 - 241; *Industrial Strength Solutions*, pages 24, 68, 74, 79, 95 - 103, 112 - 115, 147, 182 - 188, 203, 277; *Core Teams Work*, pages 15 - 17, 19 - 24, 43, 46 - 50, 57, 76 - 108, 113 - 117, 172 - 179, 183, 212 – 216, 220 - 226.)

Questions for your team: Which of the issues above are the ones your team addresses most often and why? Which of the 21 issues are problem areas that need to be openly and positively confronted by your core team? What are the values displayed when the issues are handled well? What values are violated when they are not addressed or handled poorly?

Relationship, Operational Structure Analysis (ROSA)

Copyright 2019 Glen Aubrey
All Rights Reserved.

CTRG uses our ROSA analysis tool to help core teams determine how much they want to improve and who will "own" their processes of improvement. Use of ROSA is much like subjecting a team, regardless of size, to an MRI — it will or can help determine the health or dysfunction, or both, of the team's structure and activity.

We share this with you here to assist you. It is up to you to implement ROSA as you see fit.

ROSA is composed of several key elements. The first is a series of confidential interviews where three groups of questions are posed and explicit notes are taken:

1. First Questions: What about our team and operations do you believe are going well? What do you celebrate about what we do and how we do it?
2. Second Questions: What do we need to fix? What situations do you think need to be addressed, confronted, and repaired?
3. Third Questions: How much a part of the solutions do you want to be? What participatory roles in solution provision and implementation do you want to play?

Following the conclusion of the interviews, the notes are reviewed and either accepted, rejected, or modified by the interviewee. We do not stop until explicit agreement exists from the interviewee and interviewer that the answers noted in fact portray the contents correctly.

Normally a ROSA interview that deals with items that we are doing right, or that "need to be fixed," represents some or many of the 21 Issues for Core Teams. In fact, we often use this list with the interviewee and interviewer to help guide our process of discussion.

Interviews are cataloged, and treated confidentially. They are not shared without explicit permission to do so. Answers are reviewed by a disinterested (not involved yet) third party, or several of them, where we look for trends — similar answers and ideas.

What we see very quickly is that the degrees of honesty regarding the answers tell us quickly the degrees of solution implementation we can project. If we have people who tell us "what's wrong" without wanting to be part of the "fix," we believe we could have a tough, perhaps impossible situation that for the time being cannot be repaired until, or unless, people on the teams want to participate in their own solution provision with the guidance and approval of leadership. They have to want to be part of the solution, or generally no solution may work.

We look for indicators that the people who recognize problems want to contribute to the solutions, no matter who gets the credit. The stronger the buy-in to solution involvement, generally the greater opportunity for success can be achieved.

The analysis portion of the operation is thorough. Responses are categorized and tallied. The analysis team (usually two or three analysts) generally does not know, because they are not told, the name, titles, or positions of the people whose responses are being analyzed and tallied. This "not knowing" and "not telling" is intentional, not to hide information, but to assure that greater weight because of title or position does not impose undue pressure or encourage "leanings" one way or the other when opinions are expressed.

Two reports are prepared. One is a Participant's Report that is shared with the entire group of interviewees, and it follows the first one which is a Leadership Report. This report may or may not contain information that can be disseminated publicly.

Note: The Leadership Report is always generated first, followed by the Participant's Report with the approval of leadership. The purpose here is to show levels of solution participation and buy-in, or not from the members of the core team.

The stronger the desire to provide solutions, the greater is the chance of positive change, again with leadership's approval.

ROSA can uncover big issues that need to be addressed and handled, items that people on the core team want to deal with, good and bad. Levels of strong desire to be part of solution provision, with guidance and approval of core team or supervisorial leadership, can pave the way to fixing many of the negative issues ROSA identifies. ROSA results can also strongly encourage positive actions to accent and build upon already positive circumstances or foundations.

We see this tool quite accurately reflecting the true degrees of health or dysfunction, or both, of a given team.

We use ROSA to tell and confront the truth. When a core team desires to own their solution provision, again with leadership's approval and guidance, superior results can be obtained.

CTRG is very careful not to cross prohibited boundaries or enter into legal discussions. We want the team to deal with what the team discovers, to the degrees possible.

No guarantees of results, good or bad, are implied from any use of ROSA. What a team chooses to do with the information that is uncovered, and the action steps that are proposed and possibly accomplished as a result of the information disseminated, are strictly unique to the team that conducted the ROSA procedure.

It is often interesting and provocative that with the passage of time, perhaps months or even years, ROSA results can be revisited by the core team. It is or can be quite beneficial to see where the team was, the changes they've made, and the positive results they have obtained.

Conversely, ROSA revisited can tell the team what attitudinal and behavioral changes still need to be made, and who wants to be involved, or should be, in more solution provision, again with guidance and approval.

Concluding:
The "Secrets" of Success Are
Calls to Action

Effective core teams work their principles and practices. Like gears that are fully engaged, their relationships and function intermesh to produce movement based on right causes. What the teams believe is evidenced in what they achieve.

Principles become practices in the methods core teams employ to fulfill their purposes of growing better people and producing superior product, in that order. These teams understand that success is defined as seeing another person achieve his or her dreams through encouragement and support. They know that the effects of building through people last far longer than the results of providing product alone.

There are no secret formulas or check lists here that, if completed automatically, produce best deliverables. Quick-fix formulas and oversimplified series of "To Do" items shrink in importance before earnest desires for diligent life-change and the hard work of applying right principles for groups that passionately seek excellence.

Great teams comprehend that the process is more important than the product, the people are more important than the function and, while perfection is not the goal, perseverance certainly is. These teams live and purpose to contribute their best from those truths.

To these great work clusters, these core teams, the so-called "secrets" of success are no longer hidden—instead, they are fully revealed. They are the values upon which a team agrees and to which its members adhere unreservedly. Core teams wholeheartedly put these principles into practice and desire to dwell in their benefits.

Consider how ready you and your team are for principled practice. Ask the members of your team, including yourself, if you want and are willing to engage in behavioral changes, if it can be shown that these will make your group more mature and productive.

If the answer to that question is "yes," then prepare to begin a lifelong process of maturing. Where principles are learned and practices lived, the lives of individuals are changed for the better. This is an exciting prospect.

Review the essential core team principles and practices. Collected below, they will remind the team who desires growth, to review them and answer their calls to action. These success principles are taken from *Leadership Is— How to Build Your Legacy, Industrial Strength Solutions Build Successful Work Teams!,* and *Core Teams Work Their Principles and Practices.* For the reader who wants to become an improved leader, a more diligent follower, or, regardless of title or position, a more productive member of his or her core team, these principles and practices are the evidences of healthy core team life.

> How ready is your team principled practice?

321 Core Team Principles and Practices

1. People are more important than what they do.
2. Relationships come before and give birth to function.
3. Relationship is defined as the decision one makes about another's success.
4. Function is the task that proves the reliability of the relationship.
5. Leadership is a choice.
6. Leadership founded on timeless principles comes to life in timely application.
7. Investment in the follower is the central nugget of truth in leadership that works and builds legacies that last.
8. Leaders wisely choose followers into whom to invest.
9. Great leadership produces duplicative results for positive and regenerating impact.
10. Leaders teach followers how to follow before they teach followers how to lead.
11. Leaders take the initiative.
12. Leaders qualify and require accountability from their own selves before expecting accountability from their followers.

13. Leadership tracks and traits are: Impact (a leader's presence), Influence (a leader's position) and Investment (a leader's person), where dependence, independence or interdependence are indicators of the kinds of leadership chosen.
14. Results are assured and commensurate with the degree and intent of investment, achieved over time.
15. Learning becomes living and communication is completed when behaviors change.
16. Leadership uses gentle invasion with permission.
17. Leaders want the best for their followers.
18. Giving and receiving are part of the same transaction.
19. Know, agree with, and adhere to your Values, Vision, Mission and Message, the "Code of Achievement."
20. Values are the principles on which a team agrees.
21. Vision is why the team exists.
22. Mission is what the team does, its methods, evaluations, corrections, rewards, and celebrations.
23. Message is the life lessons a team has learned and desires to teach.
24. Authority and Accountability are necessary components within the structure of a core team.
25. Four Questions are essential to each team member's understanding of himself or herself, and are parts of relational investment.
26. Question #1 ("Four Questions"): Who are you at your core? This is a question of Values.
27. Question #2 ("Four Questions"): What are you called to accomplish? This is a question of Vision.

28. Question #3 ("Four Questions"): What do you want? This is a question of Mission.
29. Question #4 ("Four Questions"): Whom will you impact? This is a question of Message.
30. Victimization or victory: living in either is a choice.
31. Choosing victimization is the decision to live within a state where an individual stays within walls of insecurity that problems cause, using these walls as excuses to not mature through the problems by confronting them.
32. Victory is a state of being where chosen character rises above circumstance and history, learns from the past, and presses forward.
33. People of victory are people who persevere.
34. Victory is best seen when an individual embraces and confronts a problem or challenge head on.
35. Nurture is care and help from the outside in.
36. Support is assistance or affirmation from the inside out.
37. Function with excellence is the child of strong and enduring relationships.
38. Transfer and acceptance of ownership is proof of responsibility.
39. Open lines of communication are the hallmarks of secure people on a strong relational team that functions well.
40. Problem solving and conflict resolution techniques are practiced willfully and with dignity on a great core team.

41. Problem solving and conflict resolution is a process:
    a. Find the common ground of interest and communication…
    b. For the common good…
    c. To chart the course for the common goal…
    d. To empower everyone to share in the common gains…
    e. To achieve uncommon results.
42. Healthy core teams live in realistic expectations of results.
43. Evaluation within a specified time frame with specific indicators of achievement or failure is not an option.
44. Real-life engagement is the goal of the dedicated leader and follower.
45. Celebrations are expected, whether planned or spontaneous, and thoroughly enjoyed.
46. Great core teams recognize that challenge and change, opportunity and action, are partners in planning for the future.
47. Future planning is a part of core team living.
48. Modeling creates living examples of balanced relationship and function.
49. A Value System is a collection of true core values in real-life application.
50. A Value System is both a design for behavior and a measurement tool of effectiveness.
51. A Value System is founded on enduring principles that shall not change. The "Twelve Laws of Understanding" is a sample of a value system.

52. Law #1 ("Twelve Laws of Understanding"): Realize I am responsible for my own choices, not other's; that changing someone else's behavior is not my responsibility; rather, I need to change me.
53. Law #2 ("Twelve Laws of Understanding"): Seek to understand how the other person thinks and communicates; use his or her language.
54. Law #3 ("Twelve Laws of Understanding"): Model what I want.
55. Law #4 ("Twelve Laws of Understanding"): Set realistic limits on what is acceptable behavior.
56. Law #5 ("Twelve Laws of Understanding"): Impose these limits on myself, first.
57. Law #6 ("Twelve Laws of Understanding"): Desire the best, but prepare for difficulty; seek creative, peaceful solutions.
58. Law #7 ("Twelve Laws of Understanding"): Seek and pray for wisdom.
59. Law #8 ("Twelve Laws of Understanding"): Remember, at the right times.
60. Law #9 ("Twelve Laws of Understanding"): Encourage always.
61. Law #10 ("Twelve Laws of Understanding"): Think first, listen most, and speak seldom.
62. Law #11 ("Twelve Laws of Understanding"): Realize that growth involves change, change can mean pain, and patience on the journey is a virtue.
63. Law #12 ("Twelve Laws of Understanding"): Love. Establish meaningful relationships.

64. Objective analysis from people who care combines truth and compassion, and is a worthwhile activity.

65. Positive rewards are evidences that one reaps what is sown and that commensurate recompense over time is sure.

66. Mentoring is life-upon-life investment. It creates discipline in people who want to grow.

67. Moving people requires people who are already moving — those who are ready and desire to improve.

68. Moving people against their will is a foolish waste of resources.

69. The follower who wants to grow will let the leader know.

70. Tools to use to help another succeed: motivation and deputizing.

71. People are treasures.

72. Build the work force, don't force its work.

73. Great leaders look for people who can accomplish more than the original leader.

74. Leaving is a part of living and learning.

75. The goal of exiting is successful succession.

76. Great leadership desires to not just finish, but finish well.

77. Four Finish Lines of Success help a leader pass the baton to the most qualified succession candidate.

78. Finish Line #1 ("Four Finish Lines of Success"): Optimal Structure, Authority and Accountability, where core values are modeled, taught, and obeyed

79. Finish Line #2 ("Four Finish Lines of Success"): Operational Systems, Communication and Closure, where full disclosure is inherent in transactions consistently

80. Finish Line #3 ("Four Finish Lines of Success"): Opportunity for Selection, Nurture and Support, where truth-telling in an atmosphere of strong relationships comes from the outside in or the inside out

81. Finish Line #4 ("Four Finish Lines of Success"): Optimistic Succession, Desire and Duplication, where legacy resides in the lives of the followers who emulate their leaders and do greater works

82. Prepare your people today as though you were leaving your position tomorrow, so that when tomorrow comes, they are stronger for the experience, as you will be also.

83. The leadership run is not to the swift but to the committed and the invested.

84. Action steps must follow decisions if decisions are to become real life.

85. Dreams become reality when they are developed into desires, goals, and action steps, the Course of Attainment.

86. Time allocation is a choice.

87. Your dream is yours until you give it away.

88. Committing to action steps pushes character to demonstrate its real constitution.

89. Reality expects greater works as behavior changes and investments grow.
90. Effective leadership is costly over time, but in the right time and in the right places with the right people, sees great rewards.
91. Lead well, and build people for life.
92. The process of development is more important than the end-deliverable.
93. Any environment can be changed at any time by any people who truly desire growth in their workplace and who want to produce better environments and heightened excellence in their product.
94. I have to change, first.
95. Character is an inherent part of an individual's make up.
96. In what ways can you improve your working environment?
97. An agenda that endures in any environment will be one established on lasting principles.
98. Behaviors are choices.
99. Build an effective work group on principles and values, and build your people in the process.
100. Desire is the agent that brings diverse groups together to accomplish great things, often in spite of negative circumstances.
101. Leaders stir the pot when they teach, warn, direct, reinforce, correct, reaffirm, and congratulate their followers.

102. Telling people what's coming is the leader's responsibility.

103. Leaders light the flame when they accept heat and, at times, generate it.

104. Problems solved in high intensity moments become success markers that prepare winners to win again, fully prepared for when the next contest comes and the heat is on once more.

105. Wins come against odds, not when the opposition doesn't show.

106. Change is inevitable.

107. Leadership that commands respect is fully engaged in, and with, the people who follow, regardless of station or status.

108. Leadership whole-heartedly participates through a team's function, where strong relational values permeate understanding, and cooperation on behalf of a cause perpetuates right action.

109. Leadership is intentional and not distracted by nonessentials.

110. Leadership is complimentary.

111. Leadership is firm in its commitment toward a higher and worthwhile purpose.

112. Leadership looks for ways to make followers successful, even if it means invading.

113. Leadership is humble and submissive to a Creator and a Cause greater than self.

114. Cooperation produces superior results and likely changed lives for the better.

115. Improvement is the result of stirring information that alters the handling of circumstances, revealing new opportunities for people to become better should they so choose.
116. Incidents are events; issues are the reasons behind them.
117. Winning or whining is a choice.
118. Losers whine, and wallow in sorrow. Winners work — toward a better tomorrow.
119. With the winner, the desire for better is larger than the desire for bitter.
120. Four Decisions help the individual regardless of station or title, who wants to win, to continue his or her upward momentum.
121. Decision #1 ("Four Decisions"): Turn habits of complaining into habitats of construction.
122. Decision #2 ("Four Decisions"): Replace negative attitudes with positive solution-focused outlooks.
123. Decision #3 ("Four Decisions"): Redirect an ego-centered focus to concentrating on benefiting others.
124. Decision #4 ("Four Decisions"): Confront problems with positive planning and action steps.
125. Good change is a procedure of transformation based on information and desire for better results.
126. Leaders and group members who desire industrial strength solutions will simply not tolerate petty criticism or nitpicking.
127. There is no room in building industrial strength solutions to continually accommodate the presence of

disruptive attitudes of misaligned and malcontent people.

128. Wanton faultfinding, wasted energy, and worthless consequences are characteristics of work arena dysfunctions.

129. Wanton faultfinding, wasted energy, and worthless consequences drain a leader's creative energy and a group's solution perspectives if allowed to grow unchecked.

130. To create industrial strength solutions, the negatives, when they appear, are to be confronted within an atmosphere of constructive teaching and corrective action.

131. Work, as we understand and deal with it today, is at least this: the tangible efforts one exercises to achieve a desired result, usually accompanied by rewards of commensurate value.

132. "Work ethic" is a value-sensitive and value-inclusive term.

133. A work ethic reflects moral standing.

134. Work ethic is the moral foundation; work ethics are the actions that show agreement with, and the follow-through upon, the values inherent in the foundation.

135. "Four Standards" that a leader or organization uses to fashion its workable solutions are integrity, decision-making, commitment, and faithfulness to duty.

136. Standard #1 ("Four Standards"): Integrity, the quest for and expression of truth

137. Standard #2 ("Four Standards"): Decision-making, the choices you make that count
138. Standard #3 ("Four Standards"): Commitment, the point where decisions become actions
139. Standard #4 ("Four Standards"): Faithfulness to Duty, the proof of when a job is fulfilled well
140. A Core Team is a living and breathing entity made up of people who are committed to unalterable truths.
141. The letters of "Core" and "Team" are in spelling and sequential order of importance and application.
142. The "C" of Core stands for Consistency. Consistency is required; perseverance, not perfection, is the goal.
143. The "O" of Core represents Obedience. Obedience to shared values is the glue that holds teams together.
144. The "R" of Core signifies Relationships, the decisions by one team member to support another team member's success. Relationships are strongest when they position others to succeed.
145. The "E" of Core stands for Example. The issue is not whether a person has an example; the issue is what kind of example he or she has.
146. The "T" of Team denotes Trust. There is no team in great form and producing exemplary function without trust present and openly demonstrated. Trust, unearned and earned, is the foundation of a successful team.
147. The "E" of Team stands for the Essentials of a person's composite nature, composed of experience, education, and environment.

148. The "A" of Team represents Accountability. Accountability is consistent proof of authenticity of character and faithful contribution over the long term.

149. The "M" of Team represents Method, defined as what work is made of, how it is accomplished and rewarded. Methods and functions are the direct results of commitments to consistency, obedience, relationships, exemplary behaviors, trust, essential components of a team member's make-up, and accountability seen in faithfulness to duty.

150. Core team members will agree on the essential values of their team.

151. Great strength results where the values of the individuals intersect with the core values of the team.

152. A core team who is relationally strong in its values, including consistency, obedience, relationships, examples, trust, who understands and appreciates its essentials of composite nature, and who seeks to be authentically accountable, is in the best position to accomplish its methods well.

153. Time is an asset. The consideration is not whether it is used, but how well.

154. The term, "Core Team," represents its constitution and level of commitment.

155. The commitment level to the strength of relationships overcomes challenges of "wrong mixes" or "combinations of difficult personalities" because decisions of how working relationships work—the choices based on desires and values agreement—are

primary in importance and functionality, and are therefore unalterable, a clear demonstration of a solid work ethic.

156. You and your group should treasure uniqueness, give and make room for inclusion of variety.

157. Differences in people, including their personalities, educations, experiences and environments can become strong contributors to a work culture where genuine appreciation and respect are the rules and not the exceptions.

158. Creative combinations are celebrated as honor to one represents honor to all.

159. Three "Lights on the Heights" help core team members concentrate on most-important agendas, encouraging them not to be dissuaded from the essentials.

160. "Lights on the Heights" #1: Counting Character. Affirm goodness and right standing.

161. "Lights on the Heights" #2: Rewarding Competence. Build confidence by giving and paying more.

162. "Lights on the Heights" #3: Celebrating Choices. When results become known, have a party.

163. Achieving unified strength in any group is not automatic. Setting parameters and reaching desired levels of endurance and resiliency take dedicated efforts and a continued focus on character, competence and choice.

164. Initiative is the mark of a team that doesn't just wait for solutions; rather, it yearns for the opportunity to

engage in a process of solution provision where members create, present, and upon approval, implement solutions that work.

165. The process of initiative is strong because it includes the people that own the problem in the design and implementation of the problem's solution.

166. Strength is a condition, but it is not conditional.

167. Strength of character changes the effects of the circumstances it touches.

168. Just because strong people are present does not guarantee that their combined strengths will be mixed in such a way as to produce longevity and good working environments.

169. Strength is not conditional, is not based on positive and negative circumstances for its effectiveness or longevity. Strength is a condition that firmly withstands, regardless. Three elements should be considered in creating the most durable workable solutions: Positional Perspectives, Personnel Placements, and Performance Procedures.

170. See what you want before you start.

171. Placing people is best accomplished through a process that recognizes where they most desire involvement.

172. A deed will fulfill the need in superior fashion with exceptional results when right people are tasked with doing right jobs because those jobs align well with the passion, interest, education and experience of the person who will do the job.

173. Building industrial strength solutions requires starting with the right person who is discovered to be the best candidate, who, because of combined relational and functional qualifications, is most equipped to fulfill the jobs that need to be done.

174. Intentionally align best people first for best deliverables next, yielding fulfilled core team members who are placed correctly because they are part of the placement process.

175. Look for the right people — then assure that the job can be done. Engage in a cooperative effort to generate job descriptions that not only accomplish need, but also include right people who will perform the deed.

176. Correctly positioning people on the basis of passion and potential, character and competence, builds the kind of strengths great core teams desire.

177. Identify relational behaviors and measure them.

178. Identify functional behaviors and measure them.

179. Strong work efforts produce *tangibles,* hands-on results that are measurable.

180. Relational behaviors are constitutionally part of a category called intangibles, defined as those things which cannot be bought or sold. Instead, they are natural, inherent to character, and values-descriptive.

181. Truly powerful people exercise humility because it is part of their true essence, and in that exercise they generate power!

182. Four critical areas of relationships and operational functionality are called "Four Attributes of Industrial Strength Solutions." These are: Holistic View, Wholeness, Humility, and Firm Resolve.

183. Attribute #1 ("Four Attributes of Industrial Strength Solutions"): Holistic View, the perspective coming from the desire to see the bigger picture, seeking understanding from multiple sources and sifting information to delineate appropriate action

184. Attribute #2 ("Four Attributes of Industrial Strength Solutions"): Wholeness, a state of being characterized by living at peace with one's self and living in viable and growing relationships with others, where agreement on values is the foundation for interchange and cooperation

185. Attribute #3 ("Four Attributes of Industrial Strength Solutions"): Humility, a characteristic of character coming from the choice to prefer others before self, placing their agendas first, giving freely from one's own storehouse to assure opportunities of success

186. Attribute #4 ("Four Attributes of Industrial Strength Solutions"): Firm Resolve, declared and unwavering commitment to action, where success aligns with true values and motives, and methods exemplify an unalterable dedication to living and working in truth

187. Balance is defined as a measured equilibrium that gauges and evaluates perspective and action against an agreed standard of health.

188. Balance is the process of instituting and distributing unified weight and importance to more than one necessary element of a work mixture at the same time.

189. Balance is achieved when people not only know their limits as to how much work they should engage, but how much rest is required for harmonized existence and contribution as well.

190. Balance should be properly planned and included as an expectation of core team participation.

191. Balance promotes health and longevity, and ultimately provisions best opportunities for greater fulfillment of roles and contentment of the people who perform them.

192. The process of incorporating balance into the people of the core team develops great people as it unfolds.

193. The positive results from good decisions to achieve balance are often seen sooner as opposed to later, and potentially last a lifetime.

194. Where rest and work in correct alignment are peaceful cohabitants instead of to-the-death competitors, a person's worth is validated and opportunities for growth provided.

195. Perspectives become tried and true in challenging business environments.

196. Application of principles into real life has always been where the common rubber and roads connect.

197. Purposed change begs to be given the chance to be born and develop especially in relationships.

198. The responsibility for the person who believes change is needful rests with him or her. That individual becomes the one who takes the initiative to live it first and promote it second.

199. For change notions to become change motions, the actions coming from new ideas must conform to actions from the idea generator, first.

200. It starts with you, if you are the one who desires positive change.

201. Design and use a Strategic Plan whose successful implementation will serve as proof that the changes you deem needful can be done.

202. If positive change is desired it must be first acquired within the one who wants it the most.

203. When desire, based on dedicated doctrine, outweighs difficult and disturbing distractions, its decisive action declares that truth, in real life, works.

204. The one who takes the initiative becomes the point person of proof.

205. The process of creating a workable solution that contributes to industrial strength will be more important than the product, and will use time as an ally, not an opponent.

206. Unwavering assurance in best outcomes gives cause for endurance when challenges increase.

207. People who want best outcomes will see change productivity as a result of best practices, they themselves becoming the authors and finishers.

208. Results and rewards come to the one who sees change as needful and willfully and willingly alters his or her person, first.

209. Followers and core team members know that when sought-after changes work first in themselves, they cause waves of better attitudes, aptitudes, and actions from others.

210. Those who rise from lesser to greater character may not be people on whom accolades are poured. Yet, those whose conquests consist of taming their inmost struggles are the truest of persons revered, restored.

211. Core teams that comprise workable solutions invade negatives with perspectives born of what can be, not what isn't.

212. Desire forms dedicated actions and, ultimately, destiny.

213. It all begins with desire. If you want to create and be part of an industrial strength solution, act. Use your strength of character to decide to change yourself, first. Others will notice, some will support, many will admire, and a few will join. Work with them.

214. "Will you engage and become an ingredient in the creation of success mixtures on your team?" Let's see.

215. Start well, establish strong relationships, and confront fresh but unfamiliar atmospheres, attitudes, circumstances, and controls with positive intentionality, giving your best and succeeding.

216. A great team is good because it is true — to itself, its principles, and the decisions of the people on the team that promote best practices.
217. Involvement on a core team that fits the description of health is not automatic nor should it ever be assumed.
218. Great core teams work well because they are composed of growing people, firmly convinced that achieving leadership, team creation, and cooperation constitute ideals of completion that require diligence and hard work.
219. When what they receive endures beyond the price the team paid to realize its dreams, they've won.
220. Strong bridges are constructed between a value and its corresponding validating actions when principles are intentionally learned and earnestly lived.
221. What principles and practices would you like your core team to demonstrate so that your team's work culture is altered for the better? Further, what part would *you* like to play?
222. Time, target, and treasure — these are three necessities for success.
223. Time is made up of far more than a memory of how you've spent it.
224. The time spender makes the decision of how to use it.
225. Time is an ally to those who use it with an attitude of allegiance to solid core values and the growth of the core team.
226. Effective time management will be a welcomed opportunity to prove agreement to core team ideals.

227. Targets are identifying marks of evaluation.
228. Targets must be identified and kept at the forefront of concentration—both within understanding and undertaking.
229. Desired results originate not only from possessing opportunity, but also from downright hard work to make the opportunity become reality.
230. When great people are provisioned through strong relationships and functions they should achieve monetary and other measurable gains as well as increased maturity.
231. A team without a treasure in view is a team that may work but see no reason for their labor apart from a paycheck.
232. Treasure is evidenced as both an intangible and tangible asset. What is needed is balance between the character of the intangible treasure and the compensation of the tangible one.
233. A core team that is on time, on target, and on treasure is one that performs well because it is well-formed.
234. Perspective changes the way an object is seen but doesn't alter it. Reaction to perspective is that state where decisions are made.
235. Opportunities become viable options when varied perspectives are employed as part of the process of decision making.
236. Healthy perspective discussions promote positive interaction and energizing exchanges of ideas coming from solid ideals.

237. Submission is the willful decision and its declaration to become obedient to shared core values.
238. Sacrifice is the intentional giving up of that which would otherwise impede progress, showing less interest in self-preservation and more in true investment and service reproduction.
239. Service is value-demonstrating provision that consistently seeks the receiver's best interest.
240. Constructive engagement on a team doesn't just happen. It is usually positioned by design.
241. Use the A-B-C's of constructive engagement: Affirm the people and obtain the facts. Back up to see the bigger picture. Create a solution in a timeline.
242. Honest discovery shows you that if your team desires positive change, then your team will be the authors and finishers of making the work environments better.
243. People choose the atmospheres they bring to work.
244. The micromanager, intimidator, and attention-grabber are three types of individuals who contribute to constriction on a team.
245. A secure leader promotes maturity through mentoring and coaching, teaching the follower how it is done. A strong leader encourages and assists the student to become better than the teacher in the fulfillment of the task.
246. Stress is a state of anxiety arising by degrees from inhibitors that frustrate planned experiences or from

the accumulation of factors whose appearance or consequences are outside of one's control.

247. On a healthy core team, strains can be handled best where a team's values, vision, mission, and message become prevailing, central, and solidifying truths, no matter what.

248. Changing the air where you work is more than hoping it gets purer over time. It won't unless someone takes the initiative to improve the surroundings through direct engagement. Will that person be you?

249. Use the purification grid of values, vision, mission, and message, the "Code of Achievement," to cleanse the air where you work.

250. Great leaders and dedicated followers share a commitment to do their jobs well. Quality provision is a result of this commitment. Right people desire the best and contribute from high levels of integrity.

251. Truth works, and truth wins.

252. Confidence interweaves hope and evidence.

253. Tenacious people who have confidence based on truth compose a powerful group.

254. "Clarity" is defined as seeing a course of action transparently, without obstruction. Clarity defines the project and designs the procedures.

255. "Closure" is the responsible conclusion to a process, the completion of a task, and the knowledge of its fulfillment. It is seen in quality accomplishments and the communication of the facts to the people who

need to know. Closure performs the assignments and informs the assigners.

256. Closure looks at a job's accomplishment and recognizes that while truth and tenacity might have faced sometimes insurmountable odds, at the end of the day a job was completed, a customer was satisfied, and the right people were told.

257. Truth and tenacity form frameworks of action for the core team that wants to produce the best of which it is capable.

258. Right relationships and motives encourage focused attitudes and methods.

259. Reliability describes reliance on the ability of the person tasked to perform a job. The degree of competence matches the need of the task's fulfillment.

260. When truth and tenacity are present, then reliability will be the result if the person and production are aligned correctly.

261. Pains and gains are ebb and flow partners. One exists as a balance to the other as movement toward accomplishment of worthwhile goals is made.

262. Truth and tenacity are the core characteristics of a work cluster where their code of achievement permeates the very fibers of their being and doing. A group who practices this code, because of who they are, is a Core Team.

263. A group's journey into significance combines and intertwines the journeys of the people who compose the team.

264. Greatness can't be bought — it has to be won.
265. Greatness is seen in tough, long-lasting, right choices, those that bore through defeat and overcome difficult odds, building people while conquering.
266. Love is the cornerstone characteristic that a great core team strives to live out consistently.
267. Isolationism is the enemy of enhanced productivity when it prevents communication and cooperation.
268. Rugged individualism that features marked commitment and endurance originates from, and operates best within, an environment where people are not islands unto themselves.
269. Reject isolationism's stovepipes and tear unhealthy business silos down. Replace them with across-the-board open communication, cooperation and multiple-tiered achievement. Your team will grow, sustain life, and reproduce.
270. The Circle of Rights is a standard toward which to strive and a measuring tool to evaluate success or failure, balance or imbalance. Endeavor to place the right person in the right place at the right time from the right motive, where he or she will perform the right task and obtain the right reward.
271. When you fit, your world becomes far more balanced and manageable.
272. When you fit, you know it.
273. When you don't fit you should want to create something better for yourself and your associates.

You will, if you earnestly desire to be a part of an organization that contributes from health.

274. Refuse stovepipes and silos. Replace them with people-groups who contribute out of proper placements.

275. Effective communication is an extremely important principle and practice—perhaps the most essential characteristic and evidence of core team health.

276. Communication is sharing information that promotes behavioral change, the results of which become known to appropriate parties.

277. Communication is not fully completed unless behaviors change, hopefully for the better.

278. Communication is an art.

279. Great examples of beneficial communication are good conversations, effective meetings, the process of fulfillment of assigned tasks, respecting confidentiality and obtaining permission, and the growth of your people.

280. Effective communication adheres to core team principles. It produces positive and recurring benefits when practiced consistently.

281. Your team can know it is communicating well when people mature, contribute within strengthened relationships, and provide excellent production. Doing communication right has great and enduring rewards.

282. Within the business life investment model, the staff comes first.

283. Customers are served best when the staff is served first.
284. Invest at home first.
285. Provide service to customers *through* your people, not in spite of them.
286. Teaching a staff, a core team of service providers, that they are more important than what they do, becomes a lesson these same people teach their customers: that the customers are more important than what they buy.
287. Quality customer provision requires that the people serving the customer take the initiative to do it right.
288. CTRG Customer Service Initiatives: Teach the Golden Rule, implant values into every transaction, apply your team's value system to personal and personnel dealings, declare your values to team members and customers, communicate with your target, dedicate yourself to fulfillment that proves accountability and stability, and openly demonstrate superior customer service within your team and return these best practices to the customer.
289. Set initial standards of quality relationships by showing what is expected, not just talking about it. Great leaders tell and show.
290. Treat your teams like the core teams they will become.
291. Setting high standards of relationship and function requires correction of less than desirable behaviors and reinforcement of good ones.

292. Proper submission to authority is part of determination.
293. An ego that tries to stonewall investment is not accountable and therefore will prove to be unreliable. It is dealt with upfront.
294. Innovation is part of the Strategic Plan.
295. Innovation from focused and dedicated people who are making great decisions about each other's successes will produce better methods, products, means of delivery, and heightened profit.
296. What a core team rehearses within themselves will equate to what they will perform for the people who keep them in business — their customers.
297. Learning and applying are not the same actions.
298. Victory in one circumstance is preparation for the next when a team has learned from their experience.
299. When values are identified they become truth standards that must be ratified.
300. What are the core values of your core team?
301. Core teams embody the principles the team agrees are their standards of attitude and action, to endeavor to make what is on the page become the actions that recur throughout the days.
302. Take the most direct route to accomplish resolution to an issue that must be addressed, where the people who own the problem initially own the responsibility of solving it.
303. Healthy and vibrant core group clusters enjoy solving problems through transferred ownership, not

dependent on their leader to be the exclusive originator of good ideas or plans.

304. A leader knows he or she has transferred ownership when the solutions come from, and are implemented by, the core team.

305. Core teams who have identified their values and who strive to live within their agreed value system treat their reservoir of values as both a place to draw from and a reserve to add to.

306. Values are enhanced when they are freely employed.

307. Efforts spent to help promote a follower's success will pay multiple returns in the long run if the investments are well-placed.

308. A return on investment is a tangible demonstration of a lot of hard work, confidence, and trust. This return is evidenced as part of the process of growth *throughout* the engagement.

309. When a core team invests in its people, the growth is not under the radar; it is upfront and openly celebrated. It produces enhanced work products along with improved and maturing people.

310. Where you see teams functioning from a relationship- and values-driven model, you will see maturity occurring and recurring.

311. Upon a firm, resolute declaration and agreement of values, vision, mission, and message, a great core team embraces its principles and demonstrates them in practice through investing in its people. They

produce enhanced and more excellent products, and enjoy the journey, even when conflicts arise.

312. Courtesy is one of the most tell-tale signs of health on a great core team, or within any relationship for that matter.

313. "Courtesy" is the willing attitude and corresponding action to create a place and space for another person's contributions, setting aside personal agendas for his or her benefit.

314. The courses of daily activities, whether pleasant or difficult, are the proving grounds of courtesy.

315. Active courtesy in day-to-day work environments is a true life illustration of quality relationships and functions. Teams who exercise courtesy produce solid returns on their investments — in their processes, with their people, for their benefit.

316. Make what you believe become the actions you achieve.

317. Turn ideas into intentions and intentions into accomplishments.

318. It is one thing to say and another to obey.

319. Obedience to principles can only be evidenced when behaviors change in submission to the team's agreed and shared values, vision, mission, and message.

320. When will you decide to take the principles of great core teams and make them your own, changing your behavior for the better, and how will your team know?

321. The decisions you make today determine your audience tomorrow.

Core Teams Work Their Principles and Practices is a business life investment model. This model is about making what we believe become the actions we achieve, turning ideas into intentions and intentions into accomplishments. It is one thing to say and another to obey. Obedience to principles can only be evidenced when behaviors change in submission to the team's agreed and shared values, vision, mission, and message.

The final question is: When will you decide to take the principles of great core teams and make them your own, changing your behavior for the better, and how will your team know?

Remember, the decisions you make today determine your audience tomorrow.

Acknowledgements

Core Teams Work Their Principles and Practices is a book of instructions and practical illustrations. Many people have contributed to its contents. Those who have allowed their names to be used, and their stories to be told, are business associates, friends, and family members. I offer my thanks to Jenafer Deyling, Justin Aubrey, James Patton, Curt Marshal, Jim Garlow, Judy Bowen, Mary Walker, Rob Sweet, and Steve Annis. Their examples help us to better understand how core teams work.

Creative Team Resources Group, (CTRG), www.ctrg.com, is composed of gifted and dedicated people. They are, indeed, a great core team. I offer my sincere appreciation to those who have contributed to the formation and completion of this book in editing, scheduling, review, and encouragement: Among these people are Jordan Peck, Heather Hoffman, and Jeff Goble. Plus I want to thank my son, Justin, for his incredible design for the cover.

As I stated in the Acknowledgments portion of ***Industrial Strength Solutions***, many family members, friends, clients, and business associates could be listed as providers and encouragers. These contacts and associations down through the years have deeply enhanced our relationships and added greater meaning to our lives.

This fact is truer, the list even longer with the completion of *Core Teams Work Their Principles and Practices.*

This book is the product of **Creative Team Publishing**. Please visit www.creativeteampublishing.com. We are indebted to Gary Kirk for his initial advice and assistance in the book's publication.

We are also deeply indebted to Randy Beck, www.mydomaintools.com, for his website design, creativity, friendship, and maintenance. He is gifted artist who is responsible for most of the book websites on www.CreativeTeamPublishing.com.

Core Teams Work Their Principles and Practices is a book that stands alongside *Leadership Is— How to Build Your Legacy* and *Industrial Strength Solutions Build Successful Work Teams!* These books are designed to be combined, because together they help you and your organization grow in right and profitable ways, building you, your people, and your functional contributions. The goal of each book is to develop maturity on teams who want to work together well, keeping central the fundamental principles that people are more important than production, and relationships come before and give birth to function.

I want to acknowledge you, the reader. Your decision to embark on the journey of understanding and embracing the Business Life Investment Model may become a life-long enterprise, the results of which can endure far beyond what may be currently understood. Thank you for taking this journey. Remember, you are more important than what you do.

C *reative*
T *eam*
R *esources*
G *roup*

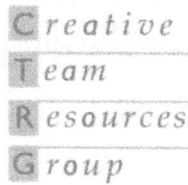

www.ctrg.com
www.creativeteampublishing.com

CTRG provides quality resources for the development of teams within organizations who desire to grow and develop their personnel and achieve greater results in product or service provision. CTRG gives people great information that allows them to make changes in how they live and work and does this through building core teams. Our resources include personnel training, seminars, counsel, one-on-one and small-group leadership coaching, books, instruction manuals, and information available through the website.

Our foundational principle is that people are more important than production and relationships precede and give definition to function. The value of a person's contributions comes from that person's inherent worth. The value of the person causes the contributions a person makes to achieve even greater results.

Contact CTRG at the websites above. We will demonstrate first-hand how our team building principles can work for you. Members of our CTRG staff are available to you and your group for speaking engagements, on-site training, and leadership coaching.

CTRG looks forward to serving and working with you!

www.ingramcontent.com/pod-product-compliance
Lightning Source LLC
Chambersburg PA
CBHW020831210326
41598CB00019B/1869